Making Three-dimensional Pictures

1 Jesus-Raphael Soto: *Relationships of Contrasting Elements*. The Tate Gallery, London

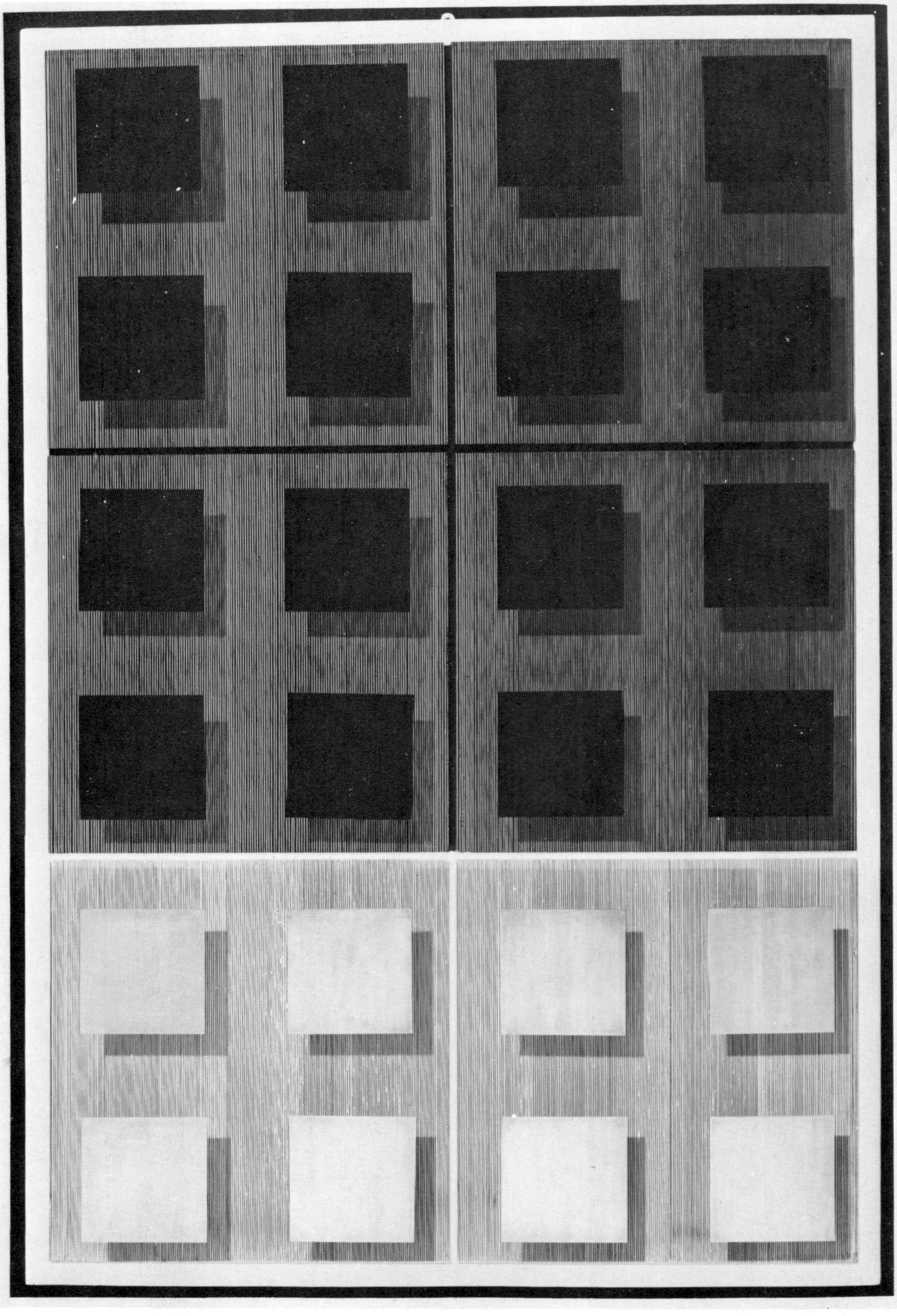

Making Three-dimensional Pictures

Robin Capon

B T Batsford Limited
London

First published 1976
ISBN 0 7134 3109 1

Printed in Great Britain by
Butler & Tanner Ltd, Frome
for the publishers
B T Batsford Limited
4 Fitzhardinge Street
London W1H 0AH

Contents

Acknowledgment

My thanks are due to the Trustees of the Tate Gallery, London for providing photographs and allowing reproduction of various works in their collection, also to Alex Reid and Lefevre Ltd for figure 99, ADAGP for figure 105, SPADEM for figure 98, The Waddington Gallery for figure 104, the British Museum for figure 35, the Victoria and Albert Museum for figure 97, Mrs Lettuce Sandford for figures 92 and 93, and the Estate of Kurt Schwitters and Marlborough Fine Art (London) Ltd for figure 61.
I also thank my editor, Thelma M Nye, for her advice and help in the preparation of this book, my wife, Patricia, for typing the manuscript, and those artists working in particular techniques who have provided examples of their work for inclusion.

Robin Capon
Maidstone 1976

Introduction

The introduction of three-dimensional shapes to the picture surface is something which may be regarded as a recent innovation. From Giotto in the early fourteenth century to the Cubist work of some six hundred years later, painters had been struggling to produce an illusion of three-dimensions on a flat, two-dimensional piece of canvas or board. During that time artists had succeeded in developing to perfection various techniques of painting, especially oil painting, and also different illusionary effects. *Trompe l'oeil* is one form of visual deception that can be used in painting; the spectator is visually tricked into believing that a surface recedes or comes forward. The painters of the Dutch flower pieces of the seventeenth century often used this technique, employing *trompe l'oeil* effects for dewdrops or insects and deceiving the spectator by clever perspective, an exact understanding of textures and tonal values and extremely accurate painting. It was perhaps logical that the flat painted surface would itself eventually become three-dimensional, being transformed by items or cut-outs impressed into the wet paint or glued to the canvas surface. In the years immediately preceding the First World War Picasso and Braque made use of a device which came to be known as *collage,* pasting materials on to the canvas or other supports. At first this was merely the introduction of reality by the inclusion in the painted picture of a newspaper heading or piece of printed cloth, but later, for some artists, the technique grew to involve all kinds of materials and became a complete substitute for painting. In a sense, the problem of depicting solid shapes on a flat surface without resorting to illusionary tricks could be solved by using real objects, a progression from illusion to reality.

Constructivism, which was mainly confined to Russia, was a movement which developed from collage. Its far-reaching influences included those on design, architecture and engineering. In the context of this book what was significant was the development of painted relief constructions made from wood, glass, sheet metal and other materials. Dadaists, Surrealists and more recently Pop artists are other groups who have experimented with the relief or three-dimensional picture surface, mainly in assemblage form, that is gluing or fixing objects to a flat backing support.

However, three-dimensional pictures are not totally confined to those important movements of the twentieth century. Carving and relief sculptures have been a pictorial device since the hunters of early civilizations scratched images of animals on the walls of their caves. There are many fine examples of such pictures in our churches and cathedrals, both in wood and stone, in carved altar-pieces, choir screens, font covers and so on.

This brief, historical outline is meant not only to set the scene but also to draw attention to ideas and movements in the history of art which may provide valuable stimuli for this kind of work. Both *painting* and *sculpture* have been mentioned. Perhaps the greatest value of creating three-dimensional pictures is that the work falls between the two clearly defined disciplines of painting and sculpture. To the one side is the flat surface of paint, to the other the free-standing sculpture. The two are overlapped by pictures which are created on a flat support but the surface of which, through some means, varies in relief and is therefore three-dimensional. This is taken as being the basic definition of the work explained and illustrated in this book. The ideas and examples therefore cover a wide range of work, from that of the shallow relief of thick paint to complex constructions in wood. Working in relief offers considerable scope, in subject matter as well as equipment, materials and techniques. Such work provides a valuable link between graphic techniques and sculpture.

If three-dimensional pictures combine the qualities of painting and sculpture then it follows they must confront the problems associated with both of these forms of expression. Design, as always, is very important: colours, shapes and proportions must be carefully considered; they need to relate to each other and at the same time must integrate and unify to form the whole. Raised parts of the design must relate to flat ones. Shadows are important and may well influence the choice of shapes and their positioning. Indeed, with some designs the shadows are the most interesting and dominant parts. With some pictures there is the added element of the relationship between materials, as well as the involvement with different tools and techniques. The materials being used to compose a picture can themselves become fascinating, sometimes to the point that this fascination overrides an attempt to design something which is more than just an interesting assemblage of unusual materials. As with creating in collage, the pitfalls are there, and it becomes extremely easy to make something of merely superficial interest.

If from this the impression is that three-dimensional pictures are confined to the intellectual élite of our *avant guard* artists then I hope the following pages will prove this false. There is tremendous scope with this work for all ages and abilities. Some of the works illustrated in this book are by notable artists, but also there are examples by children of different ages, students and adults. The work is adaptable both to experience and situation. The emphasis is on the illustrations; these have more immediacy in expressing an idea or technique than do pages of text. It should be remembered that the purpose of these illustrations is more one of visual explanation than of ultimate artistic expression. The aim of the book is therefore to show some possible areas of exploration for this work whilst concentrating on materials and techniques which may be suitably adapted to circumstance and ability. Large scale pictures may be exciting and impressive but it is not essential to work in this way, neither is it necessary to work with expensive equipment and materials. Much of the work illustrated is confined to inexpensive and easily obtained materials such as paper, cardboard, wood and polystyrene (styrofoam). To this basic list can be added almost any material which can be engraved, carved, or indented, or is simply able to be glued to a paper, cardboard, wooden or canvas support. Waste and discarded material can be used and this will include many commonplace items such as cardboard tubes, cartons, bottle tops, string, tins and offcuts of paper, wood and plastic. Adequate explanation is given in the text for each of the ideas and methods, and in addition some brief technical notes and a list of suppliers is included at the back of the book.

Inspiration is a vital part of any sort of work. A wealth of materials and equipment is to no avail unless one has ideas to express and the desire to execute them. Inspiration, of course, comes from all kinds of different places. A particular happening, whether it be visual, emotional or physical may excite one artist whilst leaving a another totally unmoved. Inspiration is a highly individual experience and one can only make some suggestions which might help with ideas for the design of three-dimensional pictures. Some sources have already been implied, particularly the work of well-known artists, and carvings and sculptures. Figure 2 shows a free-standing work by the American artist Louise Nevelson, who has used carved, turned and 'found' pieces of wood to create this exciting assemblage. Another possible source of inspiration is the man-made world, our concrete jungles, the patterns, textures and shapes made by brick or concrete structures, the facades of buildings. Look at Wells Cathedral, for example, or Centrepoint, or the Rockefeller Centre. An important point in this context is the effect of light on such surfaces. The Impressionist painter, Monet, although primarily concerned with colour, was intrigued by changes caused by different conditions of light on the facades of buildings, notably Rouen Cathedral. The importance of shadows has been mentioned and in addition it should be realised that the picture surface changes under different lighting effects, just as the shadows on a facade affect its appearance and change at different times of the day. In a way, a three-dimensional surface is not just one surface but many, as its character is affected by light and viewpoint. Inspiration might also come from a corrugated roof surface, a wicker basket, the tread on a car tyre and so on. Nature is another source of inspiration providing all sorts of surfaces to look at, a rugged cliff face, for example, or heavily textured bark. As with all forms of art it is necessary to look and to foster a sense of awareness. The materials may themselves suggest an idea or inspire a particular interpretation, as with the hedgehog in figure 64.

2 Louise Nevelson: *Gold Wall*.
The Tate Gallery, London

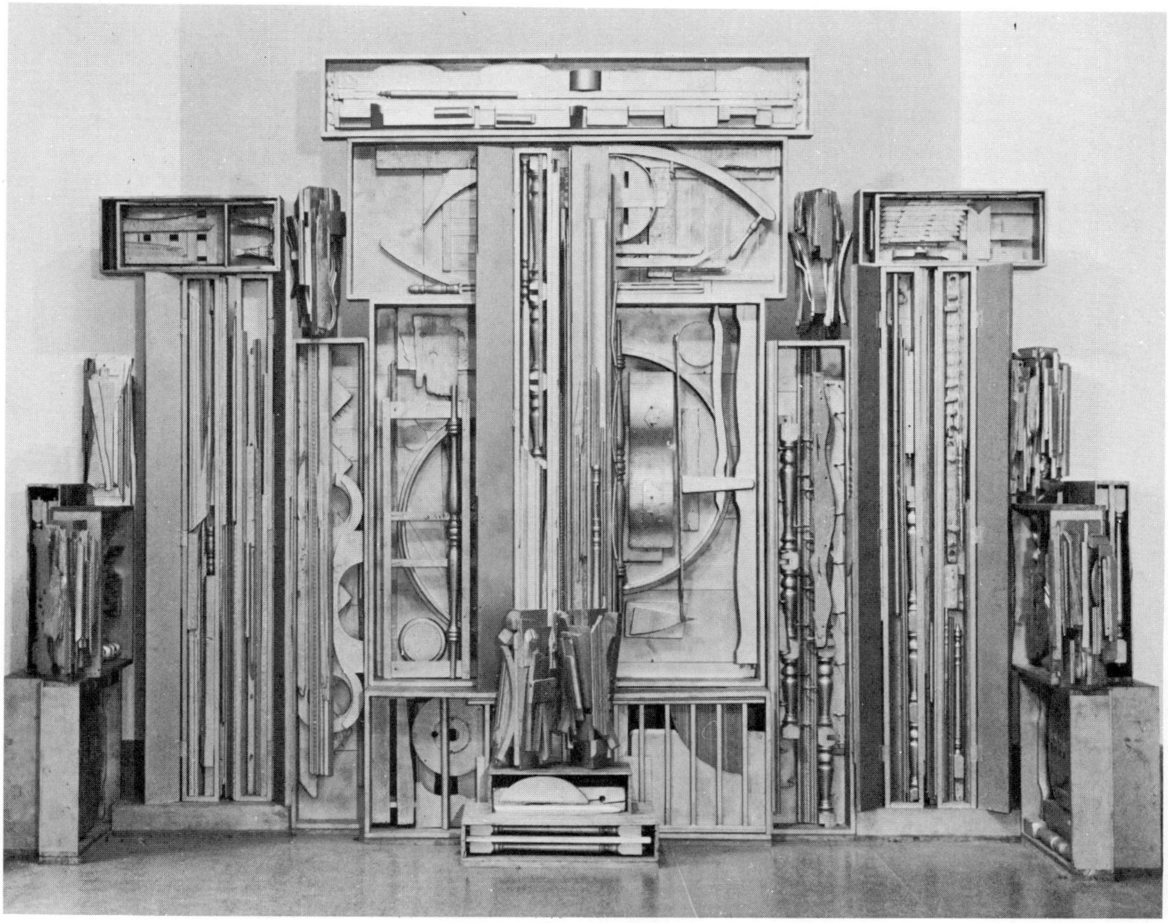

Impasto and Texture

As an introduction to working in three dimensions it is useful to consider surfaces and textures of various kinds. A stage in the transformation of the picture surface from that of flat to one of pronounced relief was the use of thick paint and sometimes the mixing of thick pigment with sand or a similar substance which would result in a course finish to the painted surface. These *impasto* or *textured* areas can be used in contrast to flat parts of the composition. The use of texture can aid traditional practises such as perspective; a textured foreground, for example, might help to achieve a sense of depth and recession in a picture by its contrast with flatter and weaker colour used elsewhere. What has become important is that the picture *surface* can have some significance, indeed, it may be as crucial to the overall effect as colour or design. From the great expressive landscape paintings of J M W Turner more than a hundred years ago, artists began to appreciate that variations in the thickness of the painted surface could be used effectively. The modern exponents of tachisme and action painting were not the first to employ unorthodox painting tools in seeking impasto and textured effects, for Turner had used palette knives and pieces of rag long before.

Visual awareness of surfaces

The need for stimulation has been mentioned and another factor of importance in introductory work is the consideration of surfaces of all types. Some surfaces can be created, others looked at and studied. Various projects and exercises can be undertaken as a practical introduction to three-dimensional work and some of these are explained and illustrated in the following text, but the necessity for visual experience should not be overlooked. Looking at different surfaces may help in stimulating original work, but also it helps in developing an awareness of structures and forms, colours, light and shade, and all the various elements which go to make up a three-dimensional surface. A close study of common surfaces such as those illustrated in figures 3 and 4 will reveal information and qualities which go unnoticed by the casual observer.

3 Texture: wood

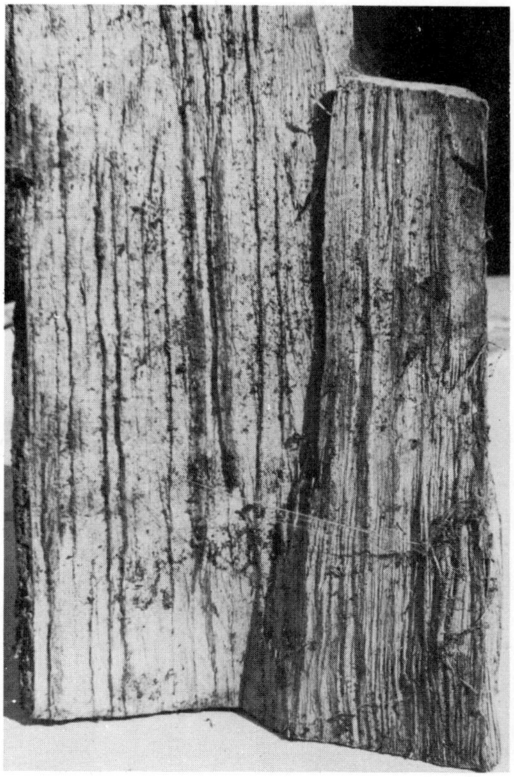

Rubbings

Textured surfaces abound and a simple and effective way of beginning to appreciate these is to take rubbings of them. Rubbings are possible from any shallow relief surface and may be taken on a variety of papers and in various media. Possibly the best results are those achieved with wax crayon, Conté or pencil on white newsprint or thin cartridge (drawing) or printing papers. Rubbings are usually most effective in black but this does not preclude experiments with colour, both of drawing media and paper. The method is to cover the texture with a sheet of paper which is then shaded over with the appropriate medium. If a stick of Conté or wax crayon is used, this should be used on its side. The direction of shading will depend on the nature of the texture; a rotary movement is often best, with gradual application of pressure. Thin paper may tear and so the work must be executed with some care.

The rubbing can be taken on textured paper and thus exploit two contrasting surfaces. A rubbing can be superimposed over a previously made drawing, design or other rubbing, perhaps in a different colour. Rubbings can be cut up and used in collage and painted work. The use of rubbings in collage form is known as 'frottage'. See figure 5.

4 Texture: wall surface

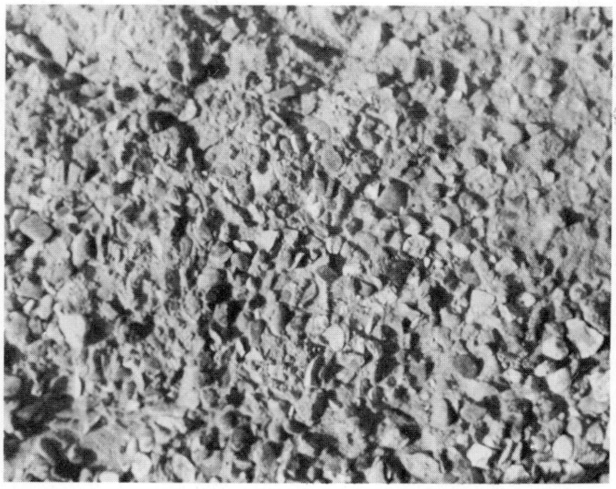

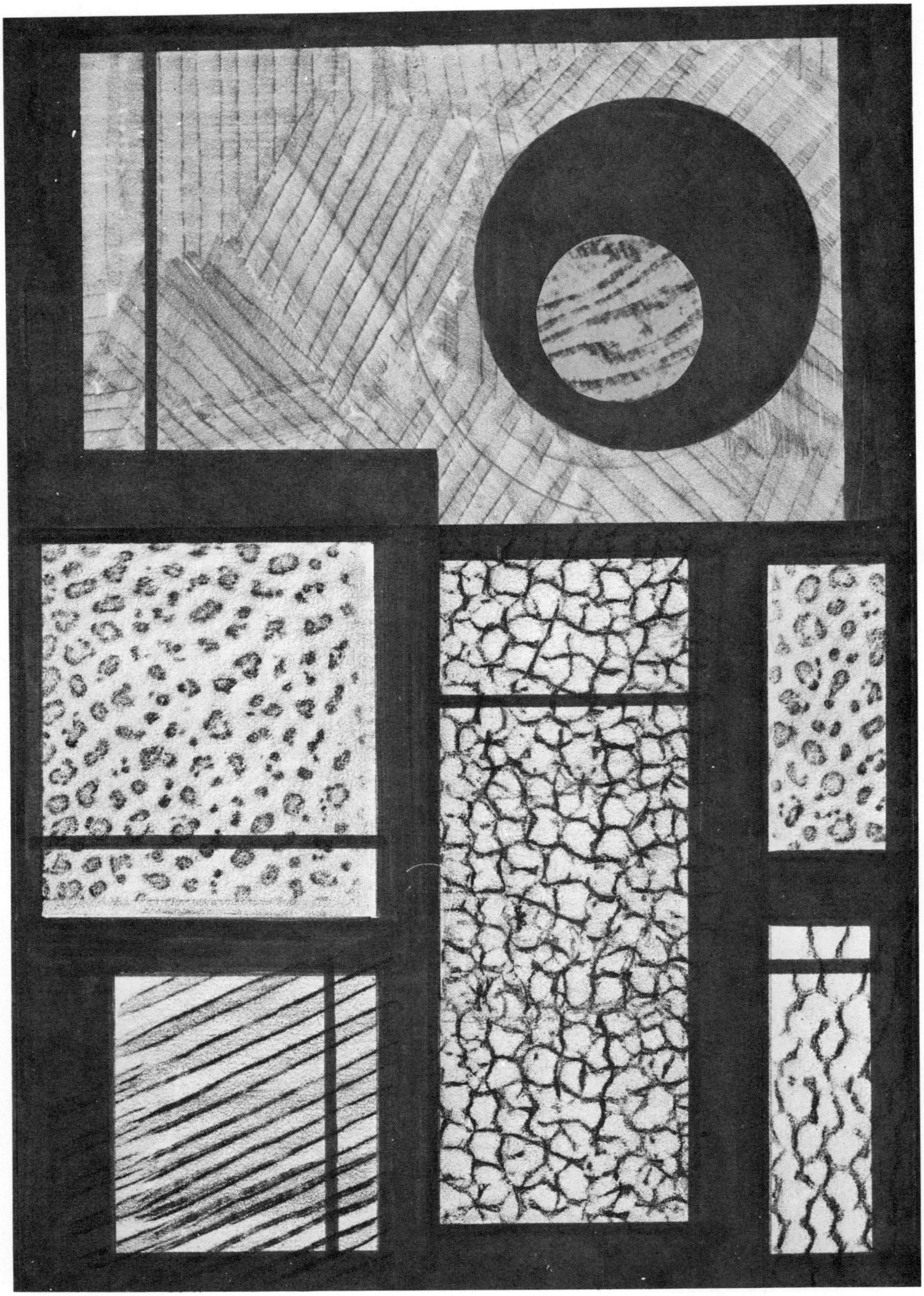

5 Frottage design

Impasto

The painted surface can itself become textured by applying to it thick paint. The paint can be applied direct from the tube, smeared on with a piece of rag, or layed on with a palette knife, length of cardboard or brush. The method of applying the paint will affect its surface character, which may be ridged, smeared, lumpy and so on. Oil paint and PVA are the most suitable for this work. Impasto is a word of Italian derivation used to describe the thickness of paint. A *heavily impasted* picture therefore is one in which the brush strokes are clearly evident or the paint is heavily ridged, as in figures 6 and 7. The impasted surface may provide a starting point for other ways of creating textures.

Scratching into a surface of thick paint, wet or dry, scraping paint away from the support or mixing in sand to coarsen the paint will each result in a textured appearance. A progression from this is to embed objects into a ground of thick paint, as illustrated in figure 8. PVA paint is especially suitable for this technique, although its quick-drying properties mean that fast work is necessary. When the paint has dried the objects are firmly set into it and three-dimensional pictures can be built up in this way, using the thick paint as a coloured ground on which to work.

The artist Alberto Burri uses similar devices in his paintings, an example being illustrated in figure 9.

Making textures

Textured surfaces can be created by using materials which can be suitably impressed into a ground of wet paint or glue. Oil paint and PVA are again recommended; PVA adhesive is versatile and will stick most materials, so too will *Copydex* and other impact adhesives. Some thought should be given to the type and strength of support to be used. Paper is generally unsuitable as it is liable to warp and wrinkle after heavy applications of glue or paint. Instead, thick cardboard, hardboard or plywood should be used. As an added precaution against warping the support can be sized, or backed with a wooden frame to strengthen it. *Polycell* or emulsion paint can be used as a substitute for size. Let the support dry out thoroughly before beginning to work on it. Preliminary planning is necessary as most of these adhesives dry quickly and it is not easy to eradicate mistakes. It is usually best to work a small area at a time by first applying a fairly generous coating of adhesive and then dropping or pressing the chosen material on to this.

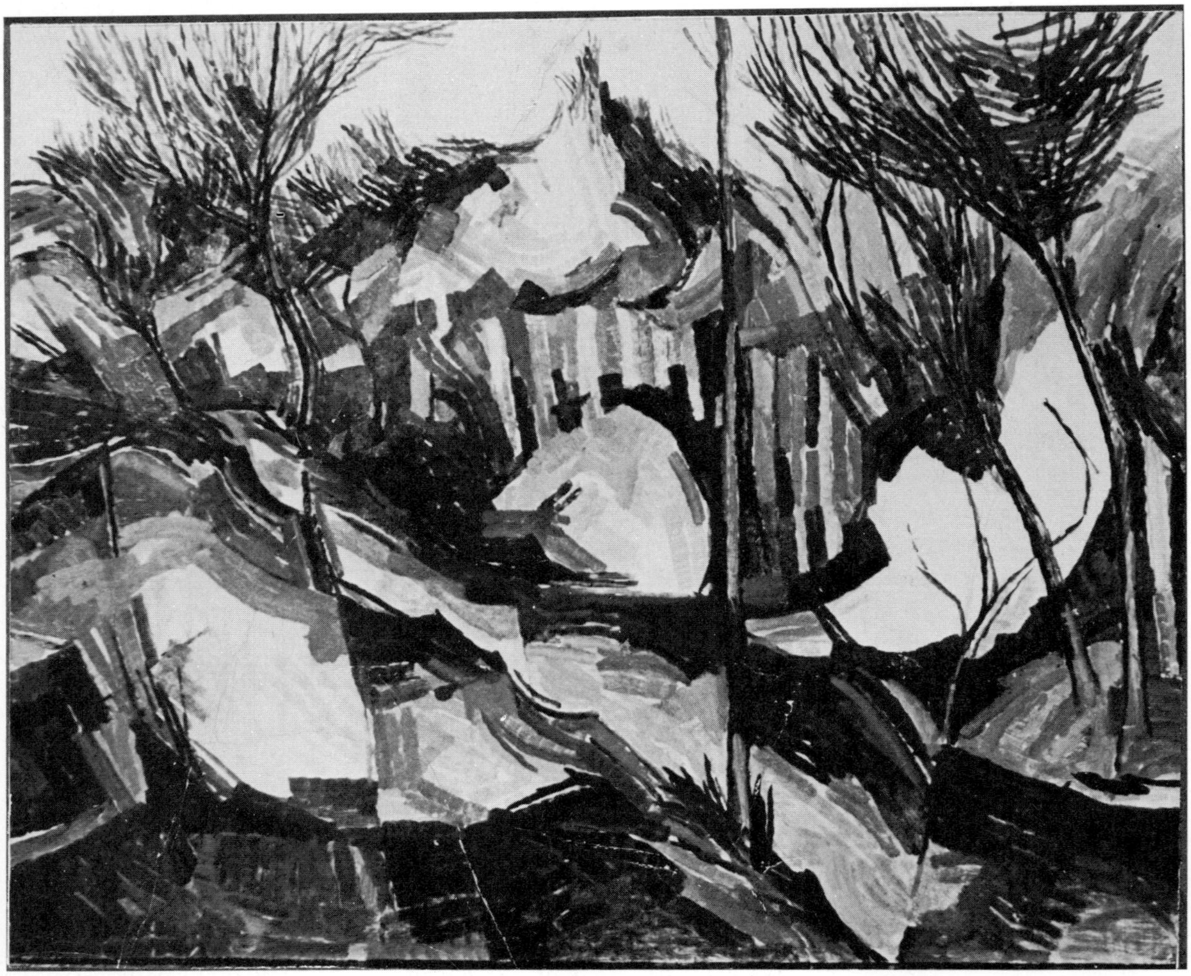

6 Impasto (thick paint) made by superimposing layers of paint which were applied with a brush. The tracks of the brush are clearly evident

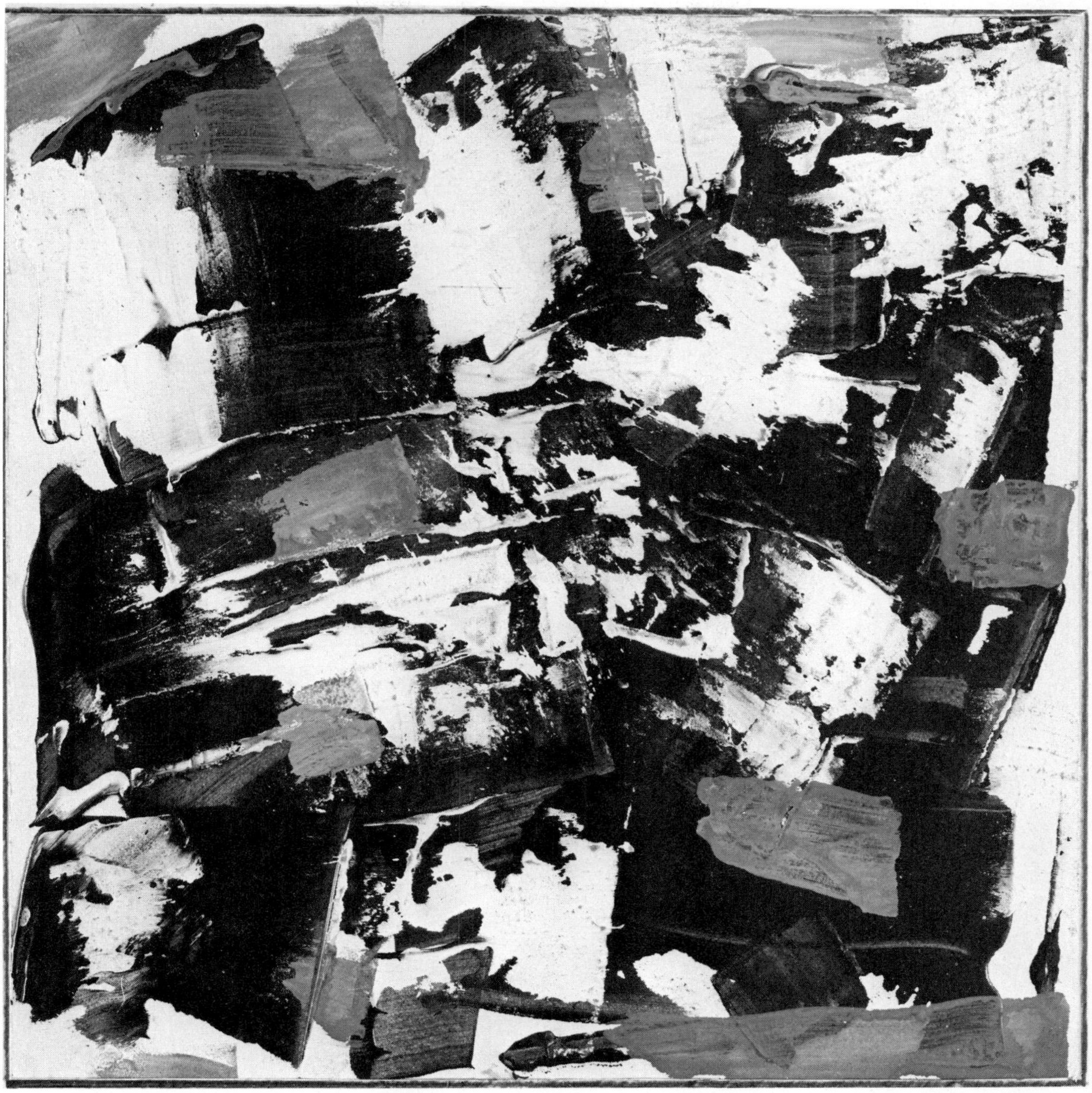

7 Thick paint applied with a palette knife and lengths of cardboard

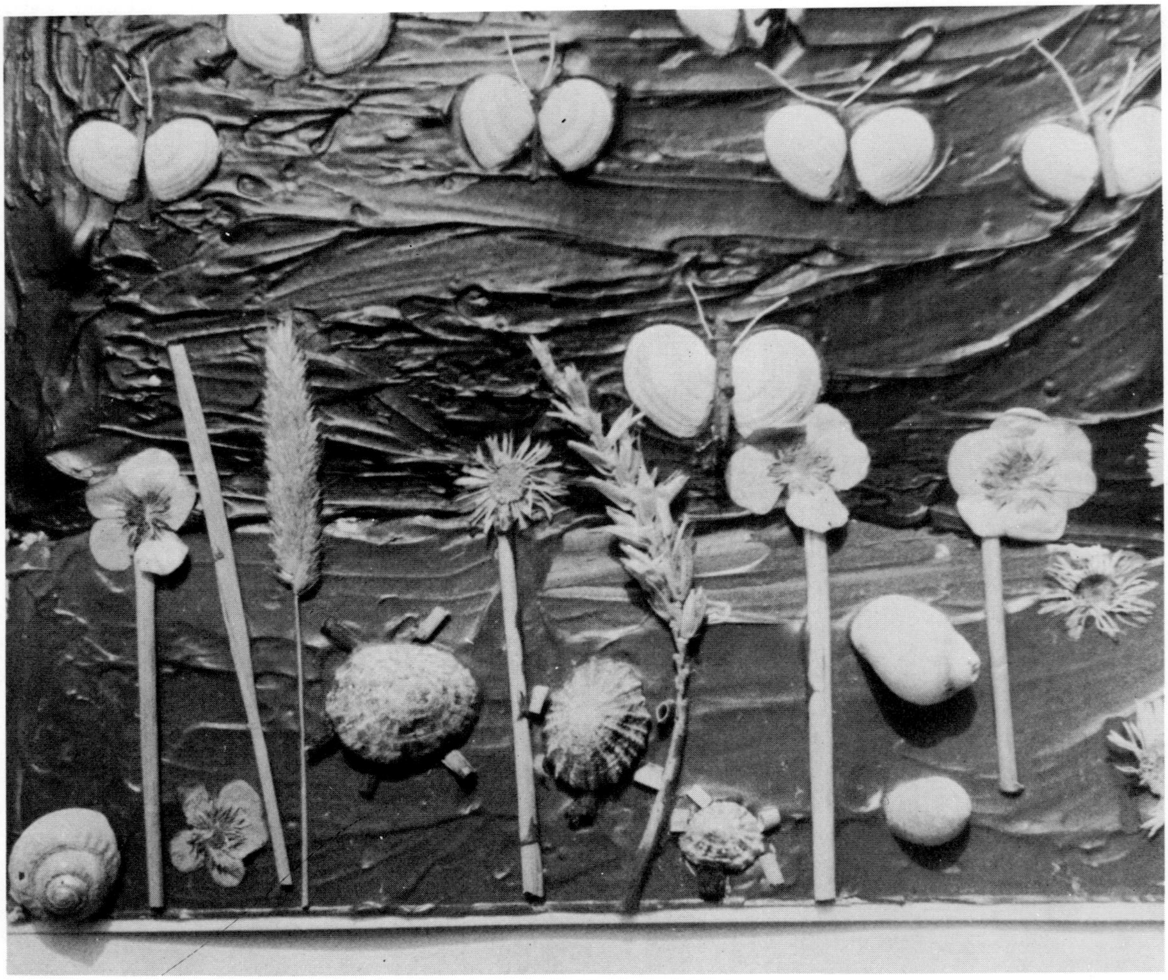

8 Found items impressed into a bed of thick textured PVA paint

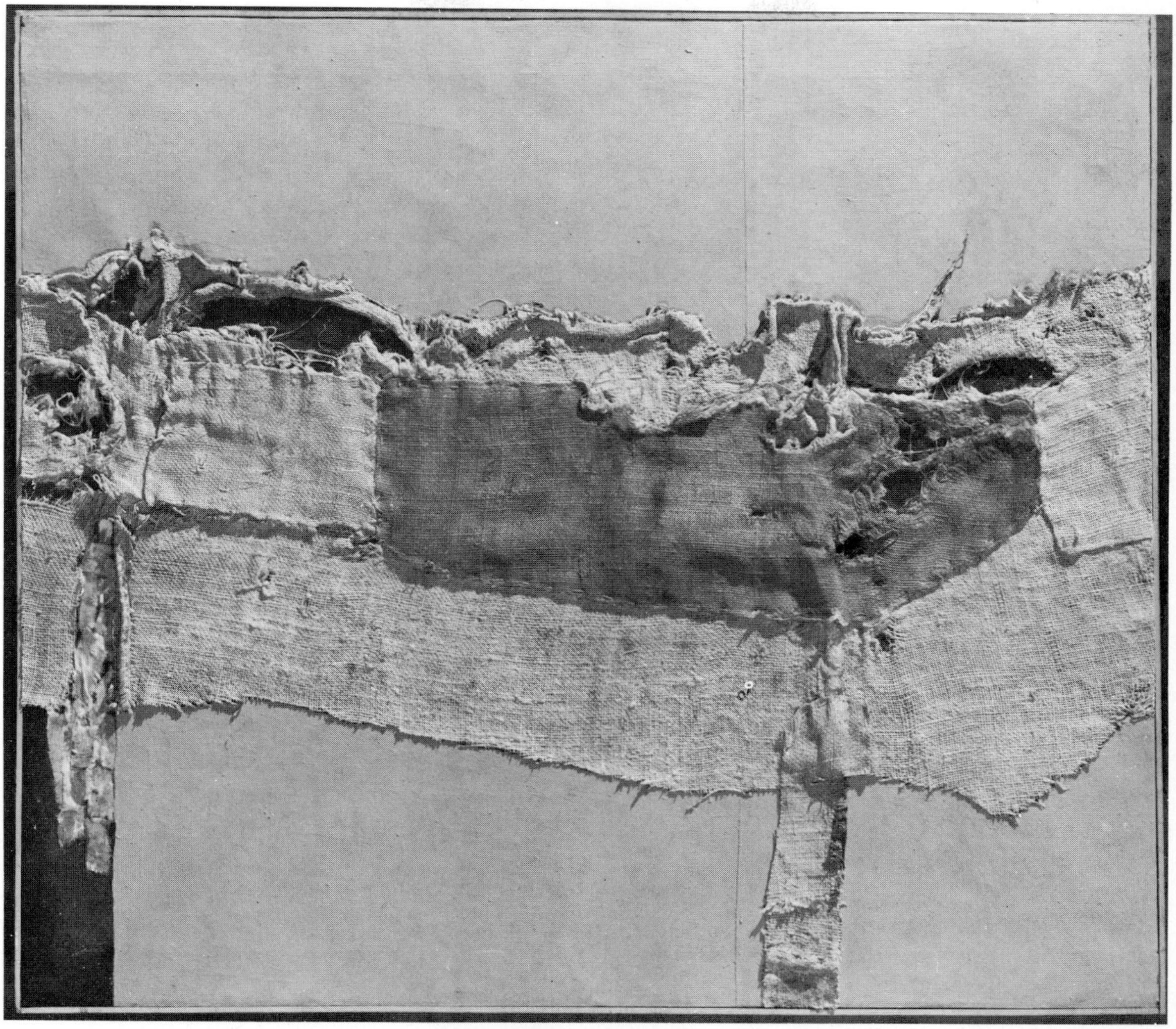

9 Alberto Burri: *Sacco E Rosso* 1954. The Tate Gallery, London

In figures 10 and 11 colour was introduced by first dyeing selected quantities of the materials different colours. A household dye such as *Dylon* can be used for this purpose. Allow the materials to dry before using them: this may take several days. Broken eggshells were used in figure 10, and sawdust in figure 11. Sand, grit and seeds are among other materials which will give a textured effect and these are illustrated in figures 12 and 13.

10 Dyed eggshells

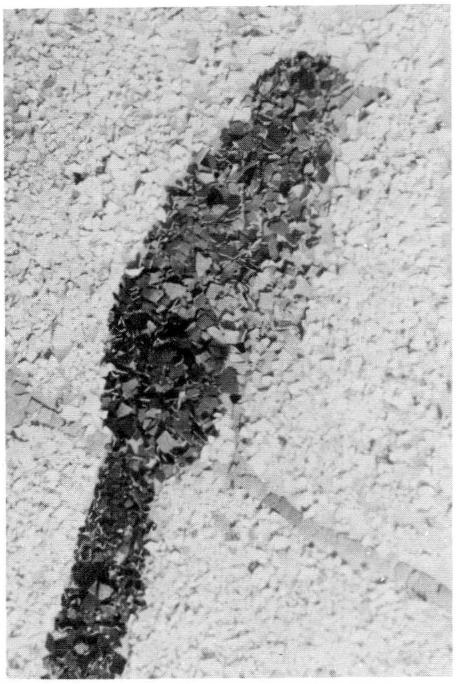

11 Sawdust

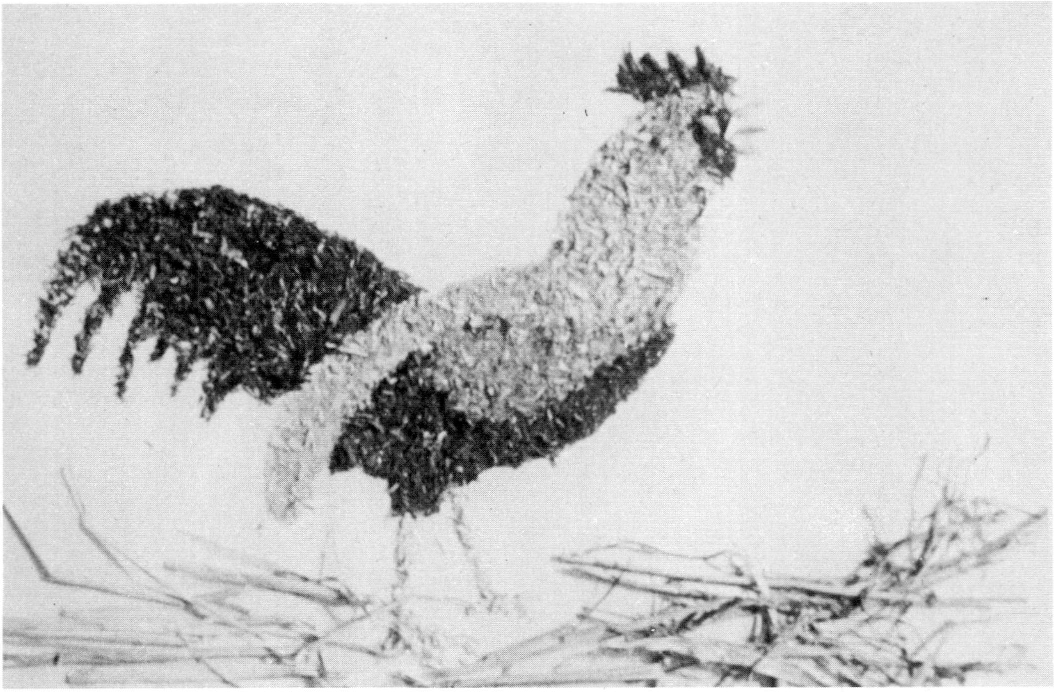

12 Sand, grit, pebbles and cardboard

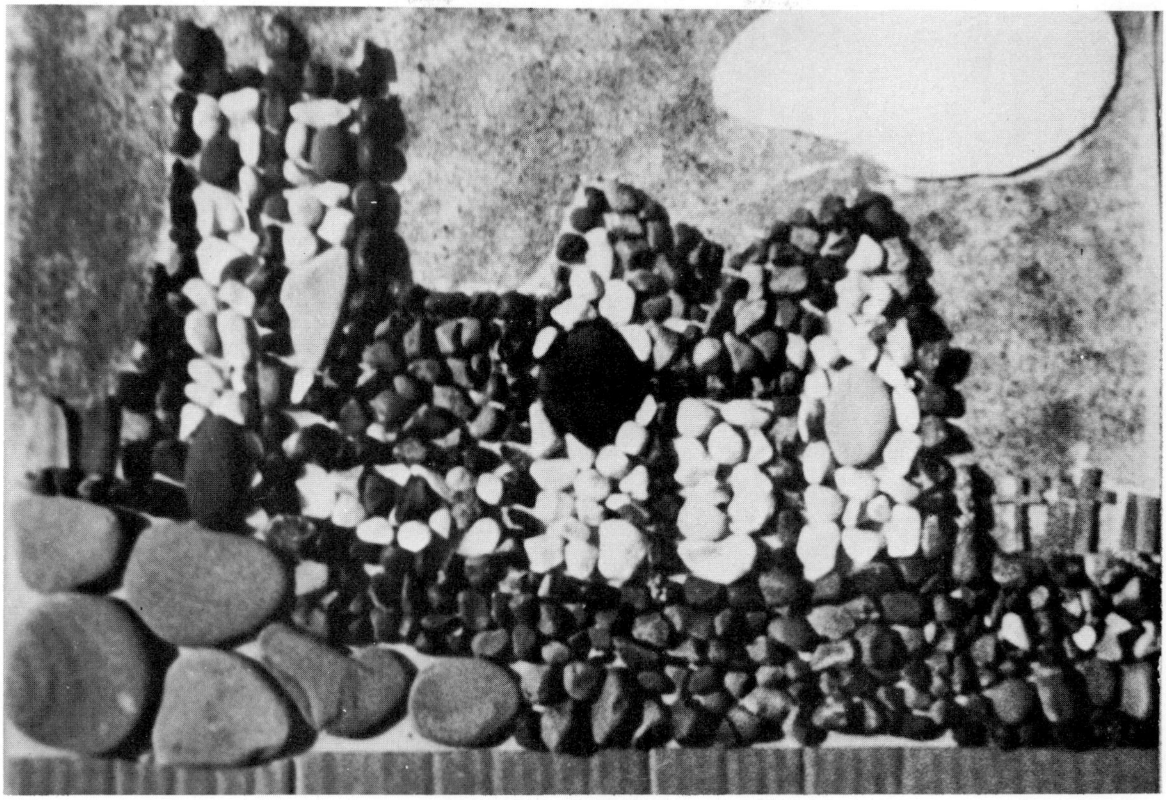

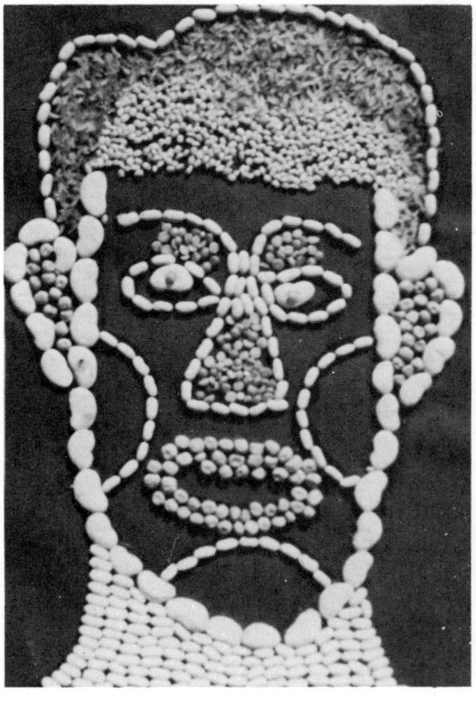

13 Seeds: boy aged 10

Paper and Cardboard

In progressing from textures to pictures which exploit greater contrasts of relief, paper and cardboard are extremely useful. Compared to many other materials, paper and cardboard are still inexpensive and easily obtained. Their use entails little in the way of equipment and additional materials. In making three-dimensional pictures in paper and card one will be confronting the problems of contrasts of relief, of light and dark, of colour and form, and this experience will be valuable before more complex work is undertaken with materials which are perhaps less easy to handle, which involve more equipment, which might demand a confident approach, and which are probably more expensive. It is always advisable if not to have made a sketch or study for the design of the picture, at least to have a plan in one's mind before beginning the work. When working on a large scale in wood or metal this 'plan' might take the form of a preliminary three-dimensional sketch made from paper or card. This is not to say that this is the only use for these materials, for, on the contrary, they can be used to create exciting three-dimensional pictures, as the illustrations on the following pages show.

There are numerous types of papers, most of them suitable for three-dimensional work. Two factors are important in the selection of paper for a particular piece of work: its colour, quality (thickness) and surface appearance in relation to other papers or materials being used in the picture, and also its suitability as a material in relation to the backing support and other materials being used. Heavy (27 kg—60 lb) drawing (cartridge) paper is ideal for work which involves a play between light and dark—the raised parts and the shadows these create. Metal foil has similar qualities but coloured paper is totally unsuitable because the colour will deaden the effect of shadows and will not enhance the subtleties of light and shade. Textured papers, for example textured wallpaper and ceiling paper, and corrugated paper are also very useful. Whilst art papers are certainly important one should not overlook waste paper as another possible source of material. Packaging material, corrugated paper wrappers, paper cartons and cardboard boxes all have a use in making three-dimensional pictures.

For relief collage work and small scale pictures built from strips or folded paper, the support (backing) need be nothing more than a sheet of thick paper or card. However, for designs which are more complex, perhaps involving layers of cardboard or built up in an assemblage fashion, then the support must be strong enough to take the weight of the materials used and not warp. For such work a support of hardboard or plywood is recommended. When large scale work is envisaged, that is something larger than say, 380 mm (15 in.) square, the hardboard may need backing with lengths of wood. The method for preparing backed hardboard supports is fully explained on page 39.

By far the most versatile glue is PVA adhesive and it is recommended for almost all the work covered in this book. PVA adhesive or medium is suitable for all papers and cardboard and it will stick many other materials as well. It is a clear adhesive which means that one can be generous in application without the risk of any surplus showing when the glue dries. It dries quickly and in comparison to other adhesives is not expensive, especially if purchased in a gallon (4·54 litre) container direct from the manufacturers (see suppliers page 96). PVA is also probably less messy than other glues and brushes and equipment are easily cleaned in either hot or cold water. It can be diluted for use as a paper varnish or paper glue, but must be used in its manufactured consistency for sticking card and other materials. Other adhesives may, of course, be used instead of PVA. Always check that the glue to be used is suitable for the particular materials. *Copydex* and '*Heavyduty*' *Polycell* will also stick paper and cardboard.

Preparation and planning are important stages in any project. Before any work is begun it is as well to check that adequate materials are available, as well as the required tools. This is especially necessary where class projects are planned. Normally in the making of a picture no individual parts need be stuck down before all of the parts are cut out and arranged on the support. Once a shape has been glued in position it may be impossible to move it. Therefore, consider the total effect of the positioning and arrangement of shapes before beginning to glue them. I have seen many fine designs completely spoilt by clumsy gluing. This again is a stage of the work which, in a classroom situation, needs special explanation and organisation.

Various ideas and techniques for making three-dimensional designs from paper and cardboard are explained and illustrated on the following pages. In the main the illustrations are not included as fine works of art but rather visual clarifications of a particular technique. The illustrations are meant to be didactically inspiring rather than awe inspiring and it is hoped they will stimulate further ideas and avenues of exploration. For convenience, the various methods and ideas are dealt with under separate headings but this does not, of course, preclude designs which involve a number of different techniques.

Creased paper

If a sheet of paper is screwed up and then straightened out its surface will become wrinkled and textured, see figure 14. Shapes can be cut or torn from paper which has been treated in this way and used to make pictures like the face illustrated in figure 15. These pictures have similar characteristics to the *bas relief* stone carvings of medieval and Renaissance times. Creased paper can be used in a similar way to a modelling material and its use is important in this context. Surfaces can be fashioned, bent and manipulated with the fingers to create certain shapes and forms. The paper will need one or two spots of glue to hold it in place. Some paper screwed into a ball can be glued to the support in areas where pronounced relief effects are envisaged. These paper 'balls' will not show when the creased paper is glued over them and they will provide valuable padding and support. If required the finished 'modelled' surface can be coated with glue or varnished to give it a more durable quality. PVA adhesive is particularly good for this. As in figure 15, the shadows may be a vital part of the work and where this quality is to be exploited white paper should be used.

14 Creased paper

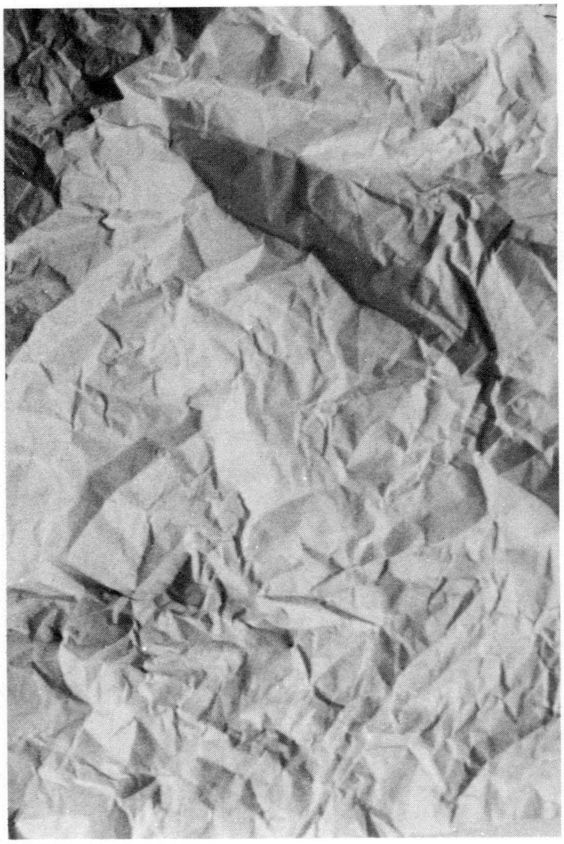

15 Using creased paper

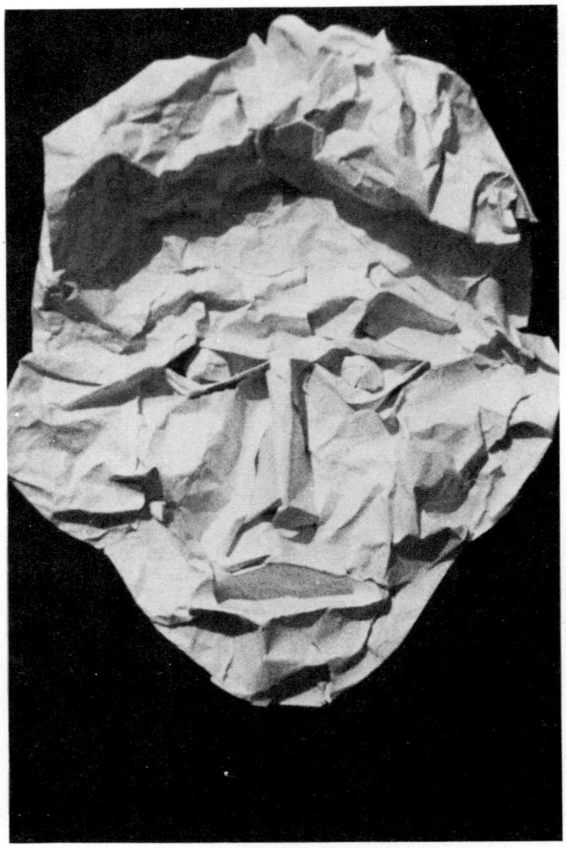

Collage using textured papers

In addition to creased paper, other manufactured and 'found' textured papers can be used for collage work. Exploring various paper surfaces by making collage pictures serves as a useful introduction to three-dimensional work in paper and cardboard.

The torn edge is used in figure 17 and, as clearly shown in the detail, figure 18, the feathery character of this creature is achieved by partially sticking down the small strips of newspaper and by over-lapping them.

16 Collage using textured papers: boy aged 12

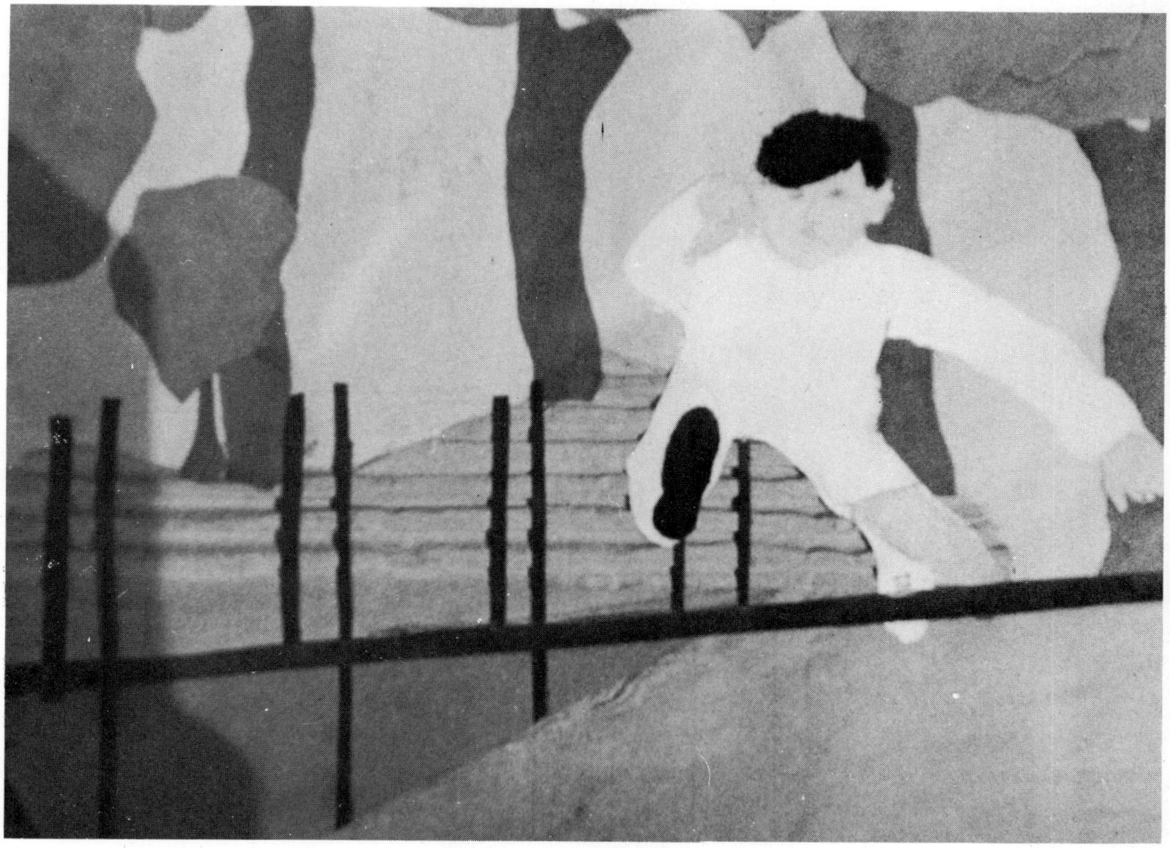

17 Collage using torn and creased papers: boy 12

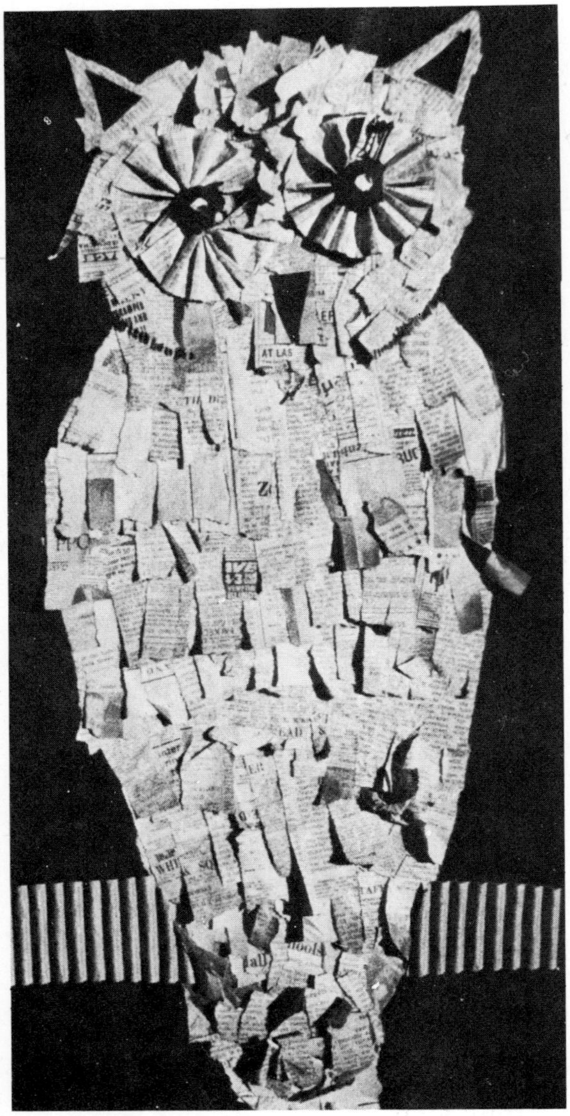

18 Detail of figure 17

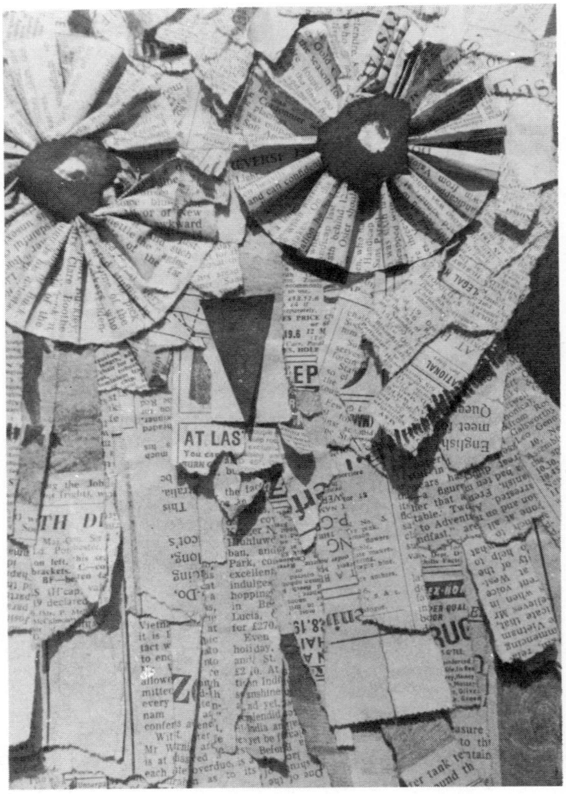

Corrugated papers

Corrugated paper and cardboard are other useful materials and these are suitable for a wide range of design techniques and exercises as well as for pictorial work. Corrugated paper is available in various colours; the grey and brown types used for packaging can be used for this work provided that they are not badly damaged. Corrugated cardboard, the type which consists of a layer of corrugated paper between two thick sheets of brown paper, can be used to build up layers of relief and also offers possibilities for designs which exploit its various layers.

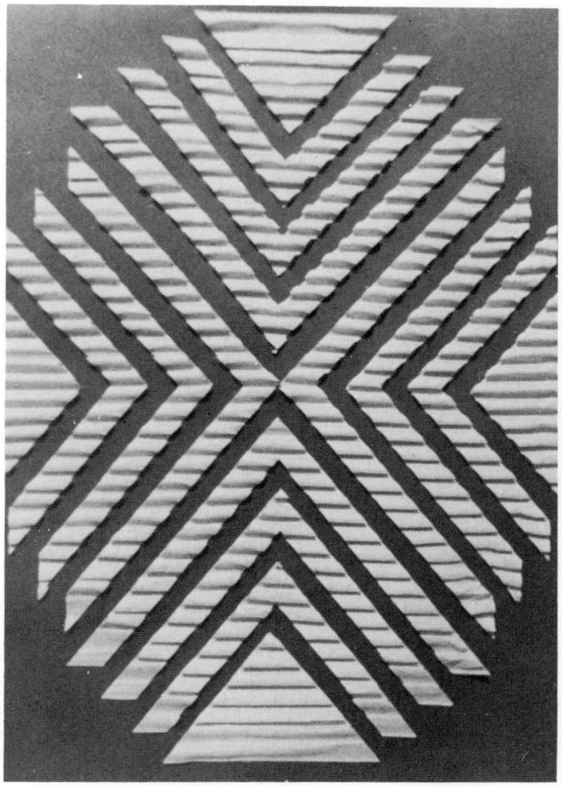
19 Extended design: corrugated paper

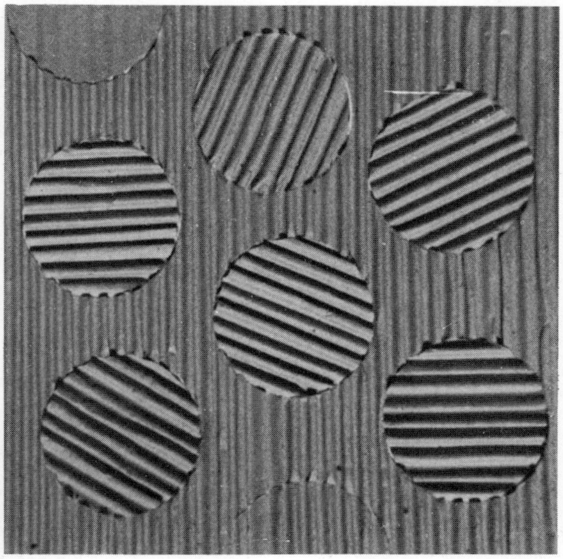
20 Rotated circles: corrugated paper

Some design exercises using corrugated paper are illustrated in figures 19 to 23. It will be obvious that numerous variations are possible. Figure 19 is an extended design cut from a rectangular sheet of paper. Spacing is an important factor here; the parts are kept in sequence as they are cut out and are merely spaced out slightly from each other. The ridged surface of corrugated paper can be exploited, as in figures 20 and 21. In figure 20 circles have been cut out and then replaced in a slightly different position before all the parts were glued to the backing paper. In figure 21 various shapes have been used, again based on changes of direction in the ridges of the paper.

Corrugated cardboard and paper have been combined in figures 22 and 23. Note the effect achieved when thin strips of corrugated cardboard are glued along one edge and thus made to protrude from the flat picture surface.

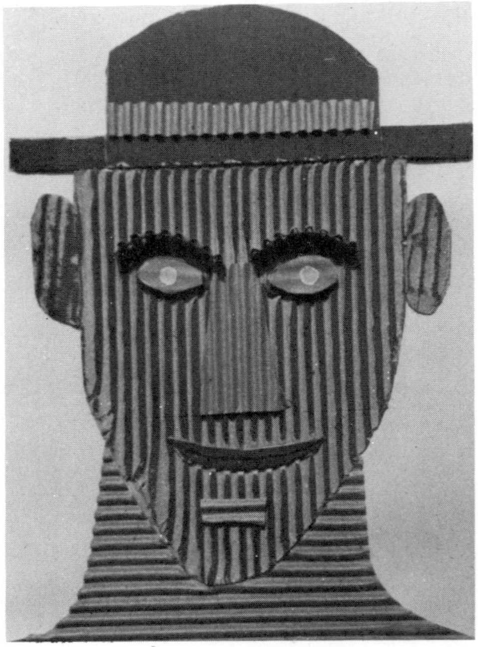

22 Corrugated paper and cardboard: boy 10

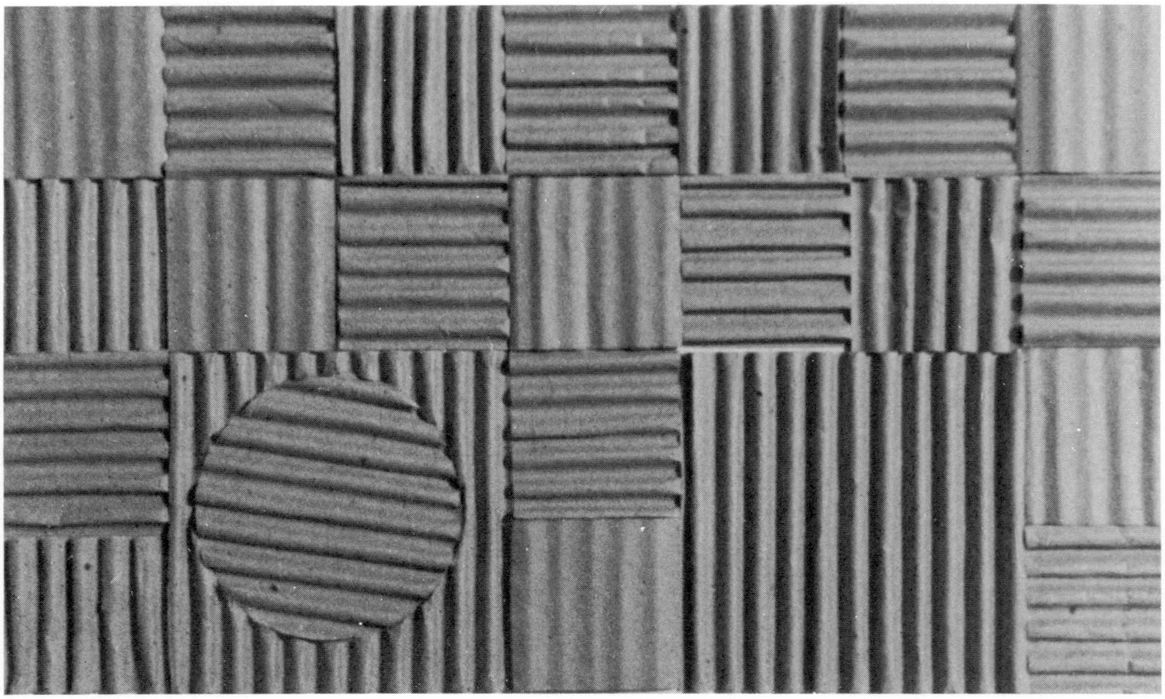

21 Design built from various shapes cut from corrugated paper

Corrugated paper is best cut with a pair of sharp scissors, cardboard with a craft knife or safety razor-blade. If straight edges are desired then use the knife against a metal ruler. Remember that knives are potentially dangerous, even in the hands of an adult. Young children should not be allowed to use knives, and older students may need careful supervision and clear instructions.

23 Corrugated paper and cardboard

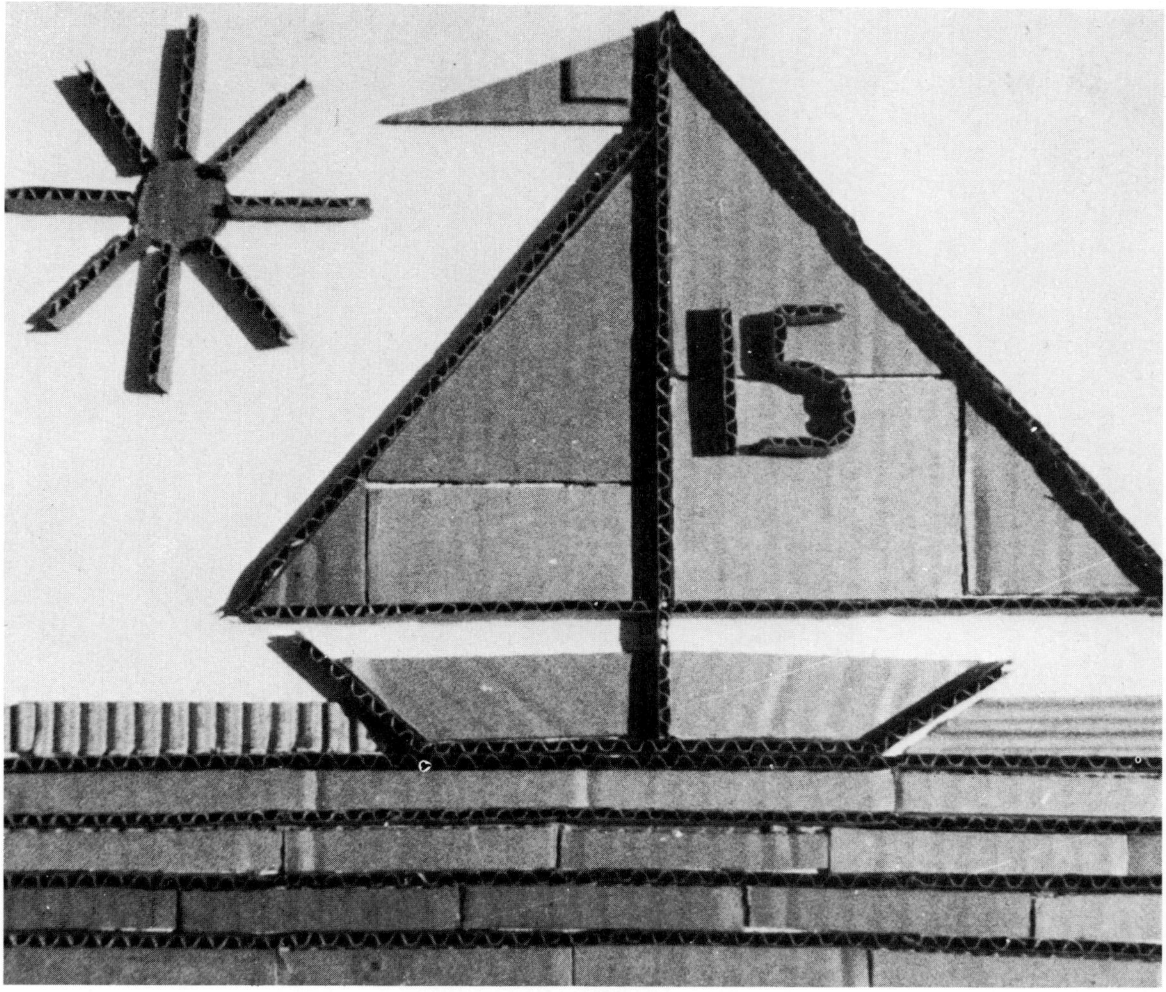

Folded paper

A simple way of making a flat piece of paper three-dimensional is to fold it. Half of the folded paper can be glued to a support, so allowing the other half to protrude from it, and, by using a collection of folded paper shapes in this way, a three-dimensional result is achieved. Figures 24 to 29 show various three-dimensional effects made by using folded paper. White cartridge (drawing) paper was used for all the examples.

Folded strips of paper were used in figure 24. The strips vary in width and length and contrasts are made in spacing and grouping. Once again shadows are of importance. Folded circles form the design in figure 25 and these are glued to a painted hardboard support.

Large sheets of paper can involve many folds and several sheets mounted on to a support of thick card or hardboard will give most interesting results, as shown in figure 26. Large sheets of folded paper may be more difficult to stick to the backing support; the folds at each end of a sheet of paper may be regarded as flaps which when glued will hold the paper in place against the background and some of the lower ridges may also need gluing in place. In figure 27 the folded paper had shapes cut from it before being glued down.

A flat paper surface can also be enlivened by cutting into it. By combining cuts with folds relief effects are possible, as illustrated in figures 28 and 29. Each of these examples was made from a single sheet of paper which was subsequently mounted on thin card.

24 Folded strips: student

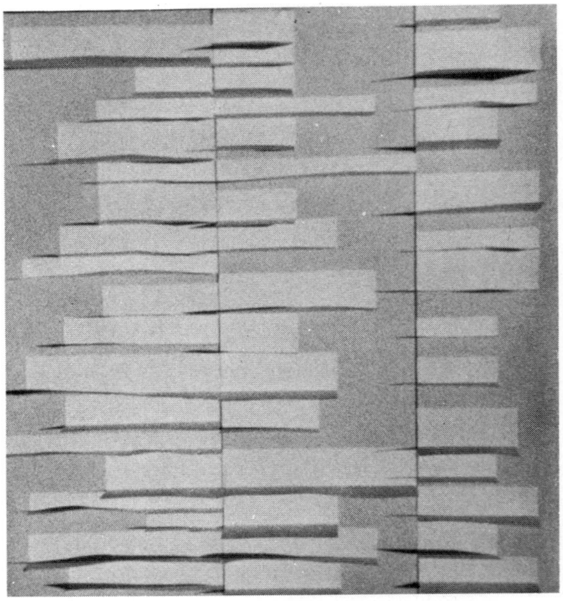

25 Folded circles: student

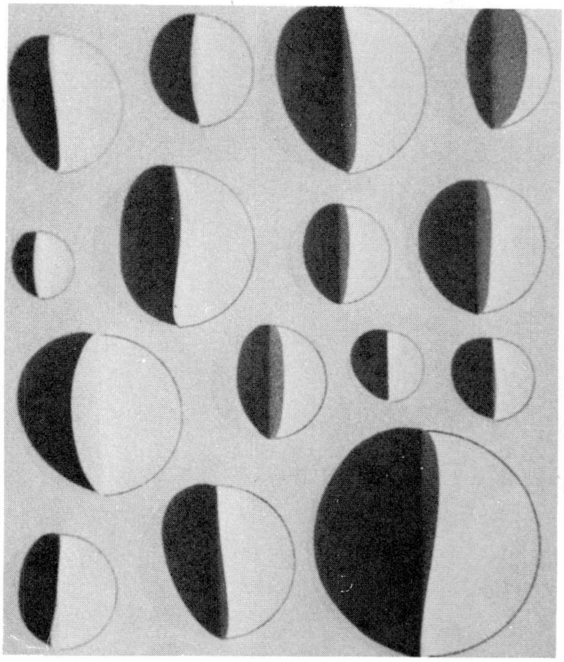

27 Folded paper: student

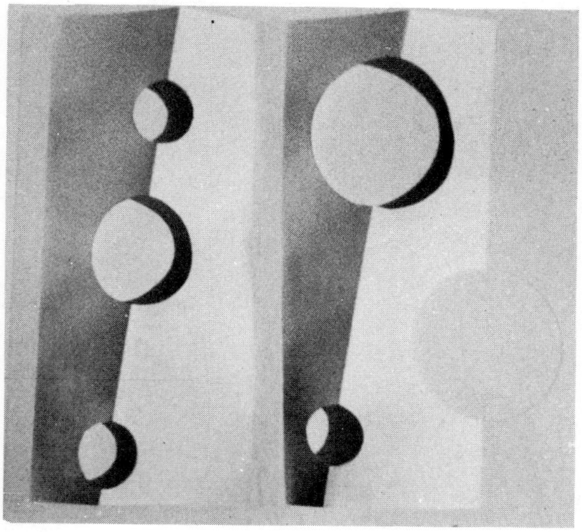

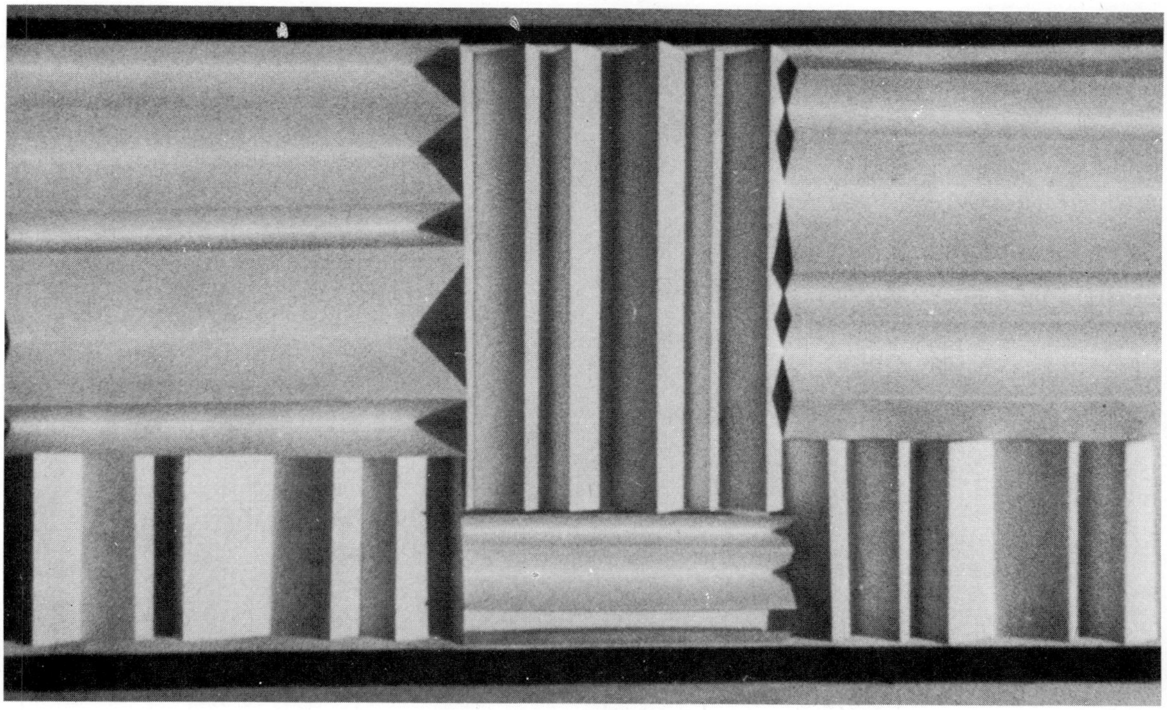

26 Folded sheets of paper: student

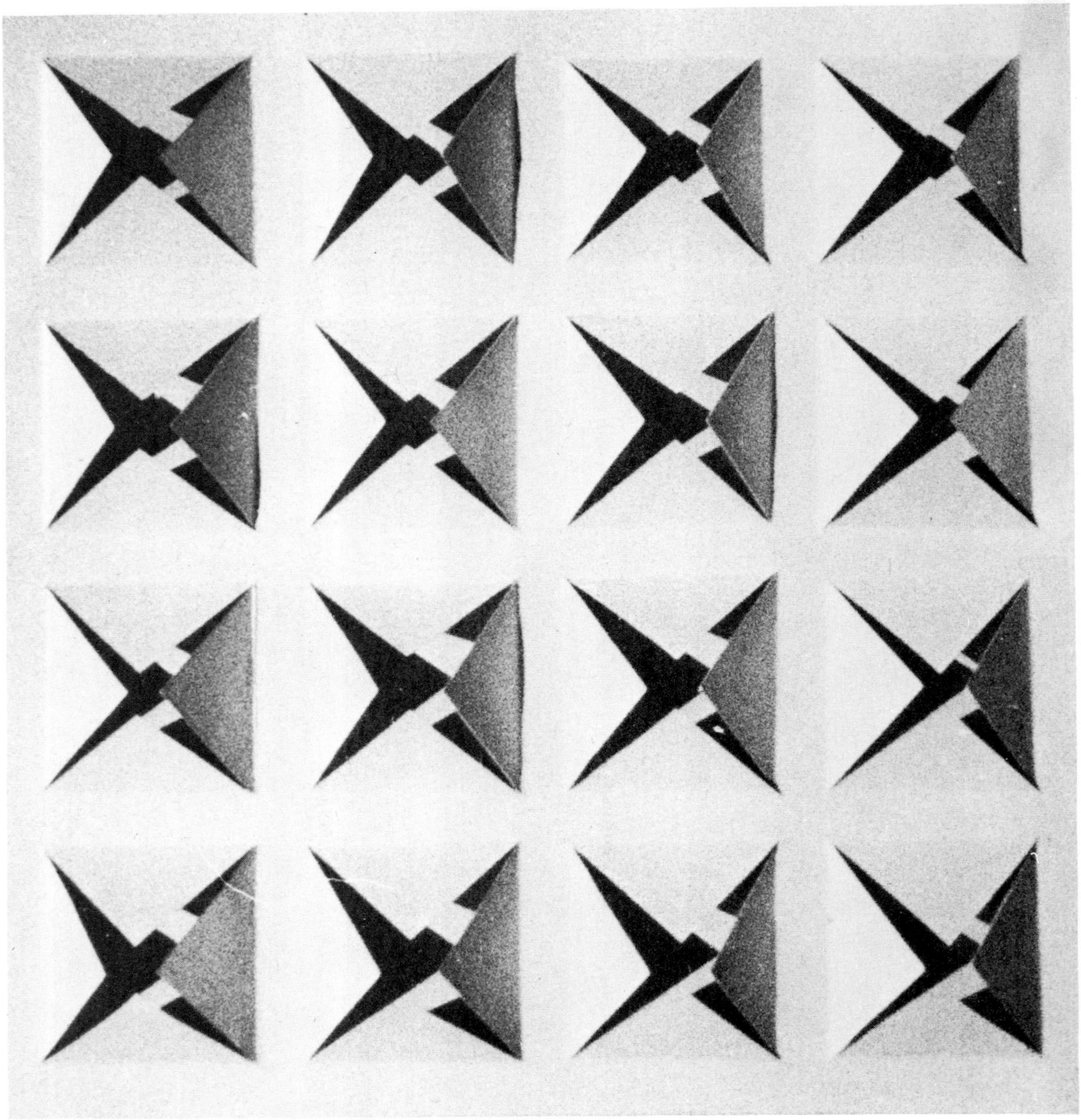

28 Cutting and folding up

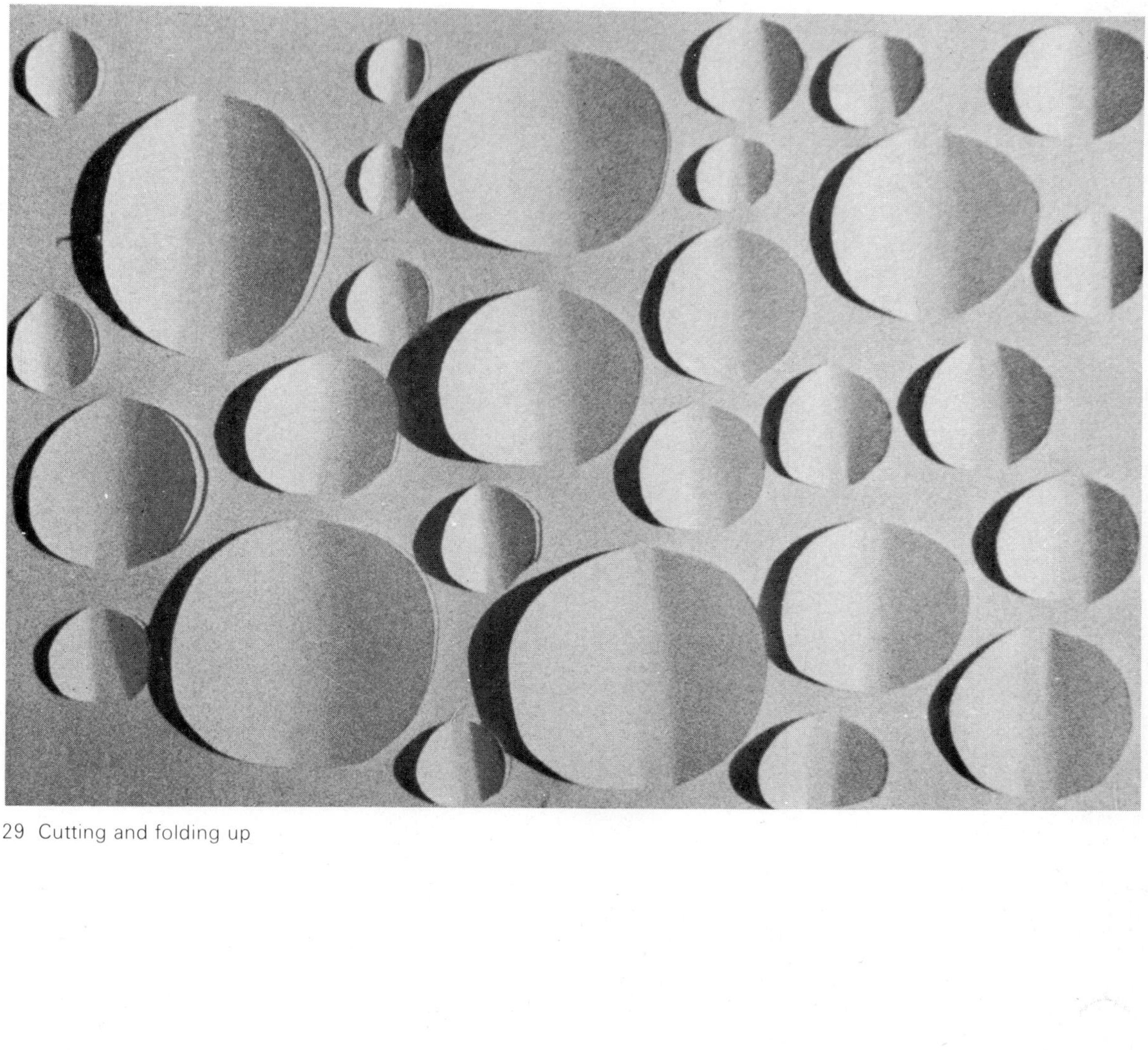

29 Cutting and folding up

Using strips of paper

Strips can be glued along one edge and therefore made to stand at right-angles to the picture surface. Different lengths and widths can be used and perhaps different colours. If the strips are cut from a variety of materials, such as paper, card, corrugated paper and corrugated cardboard, then different thicknesses will be achieved. PVA adhesive and *Copydex* are recommended for this work. It may be necessary to hold the strip in place for a short while until the glue begins to set. As the strip is held in place by a minimal amount of glue it is important that the edge of the strip is straight and the support completely flat so that maximum contact is made between the two. To ensure that the edges are straight it is best to cut the strips with a knife used against a metal ruler.

Strips can be coiled by winding them round cardboard tubing or a pencil. A round pencil can also be used to make a curved strip: hold the end of the strip of paper between the thumb and first finger of the left hand; grip the pencil in the right hand so that its blunt end protrudes between the thumb and first finger for a length which is slightly longer than the width of the strip; starting from the end held in the left hand, grip the strip between the pencil and thumb and pull the pencil to the other end of the strip. In doing this the fibres of the paper are broken down thus causing it to stretch and curve. The process may need repeating several times if an exaggerated curve is desired. Curved strips have been used in figure 30 and coiled ones in figure 32.

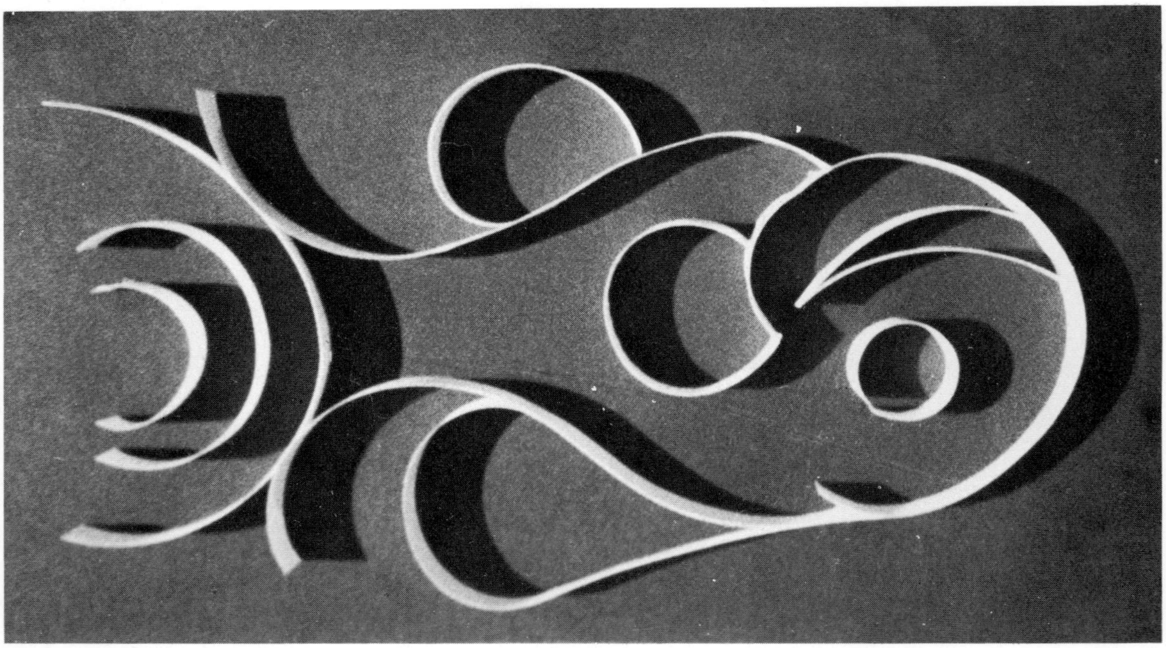

30 Building with strips of paper

31 Using strips

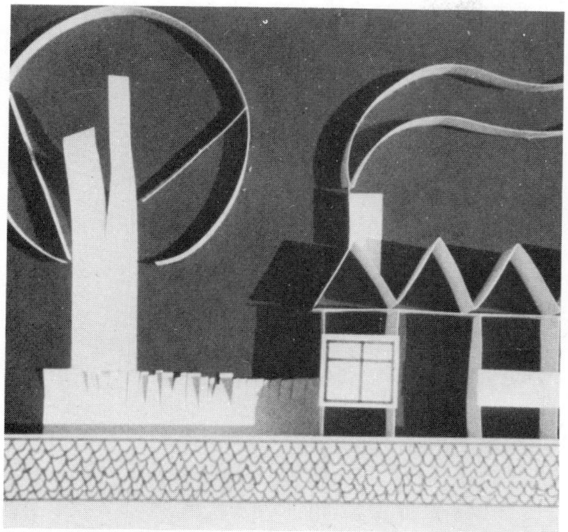

32 Coiled strips

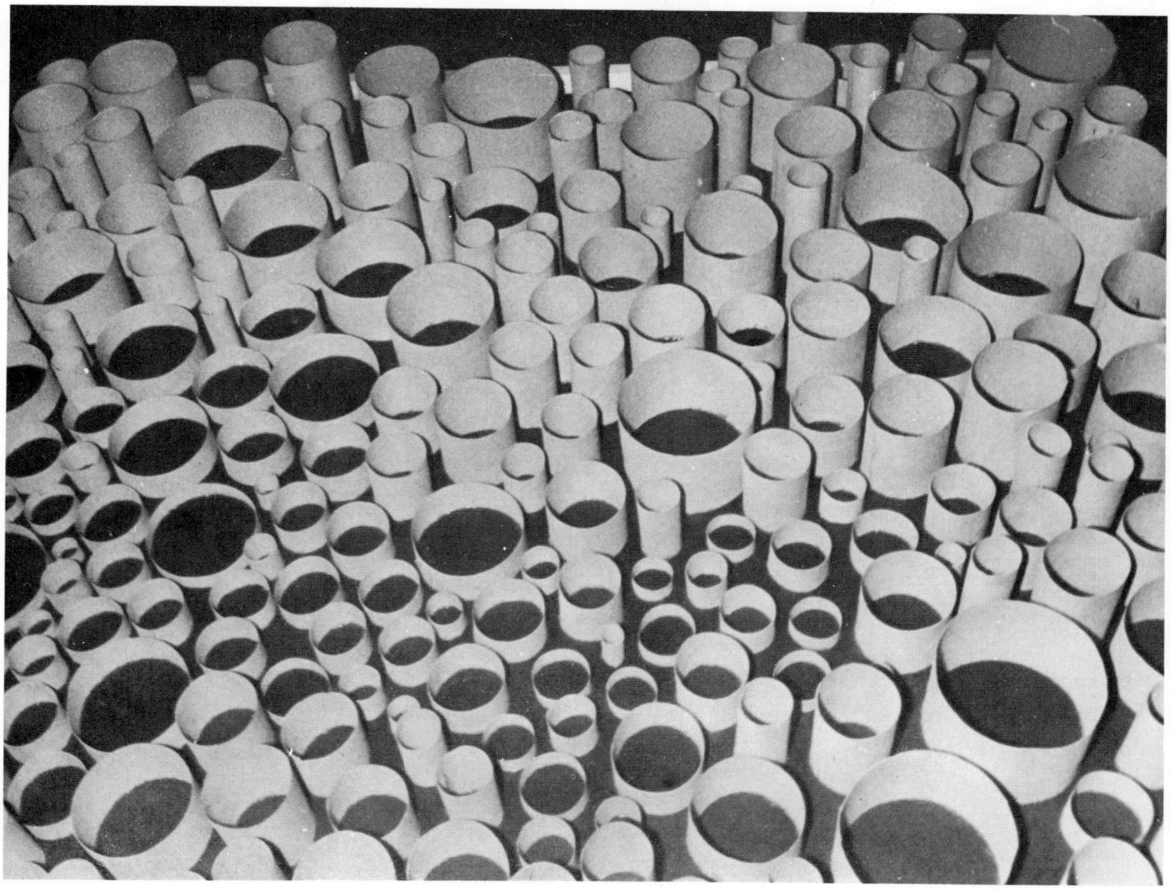

If slits are cut into a sheet of paper or card then strips can be woven through these, as shown in figures 33 and 34. Here, the straight edge need not be emphasised and the strips could be torn and interwoven. The ends of the strips are glued to the back of the support.

33 Relief by inserting strips

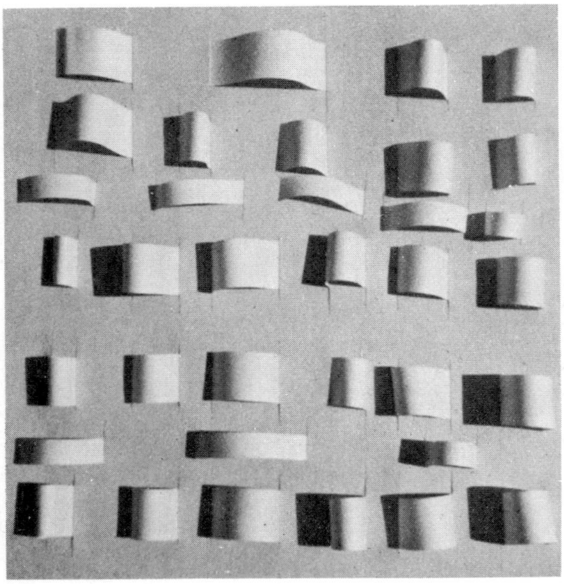

34 Inserting strips

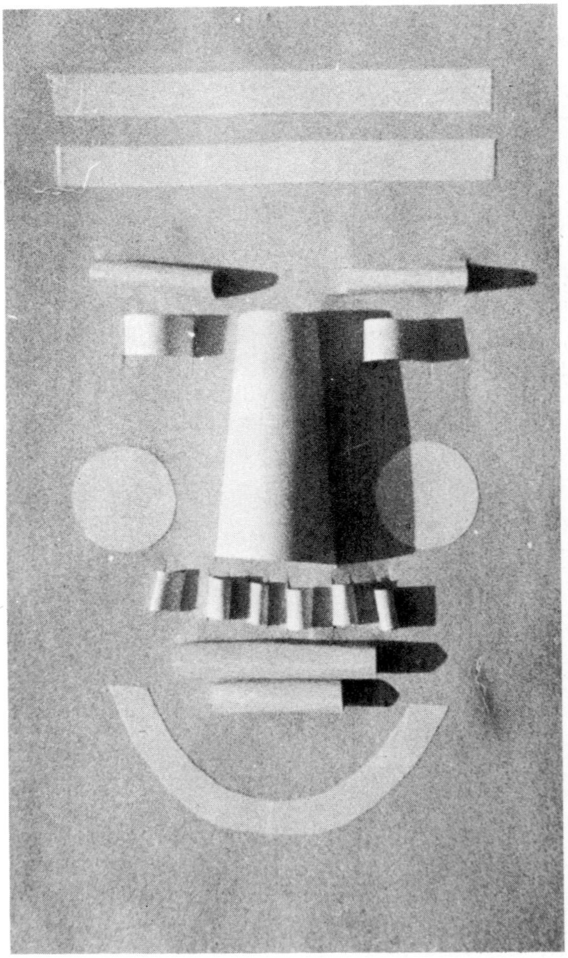

Over two hundred years ago papercutting was an accepted art form in England, made popular by the original work of Mrs Delaney and later by that of Amelia Blackburn. See figure 35. These artists used many different shades of coloured paper and built up their pictures from small slivers of paper.

35 Papercut picture by Amelia Blackburn. Eighteenth century. British Museum

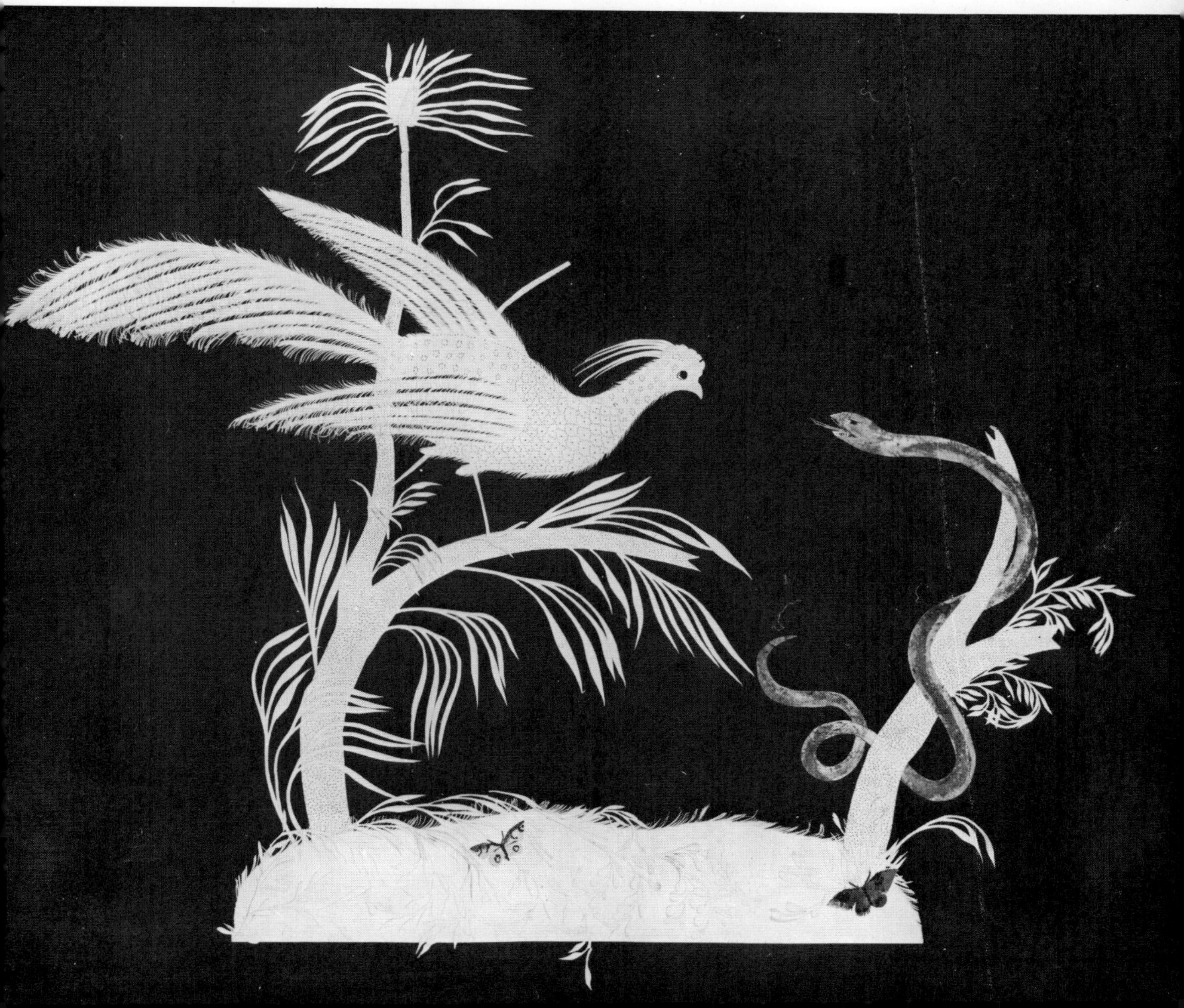

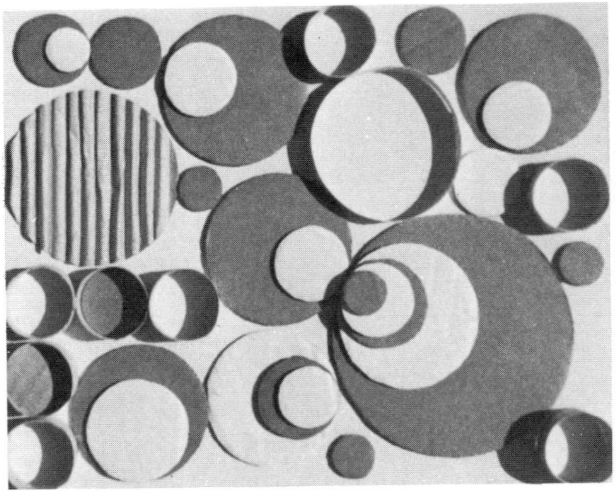

36 Layers: cardboard, paper and corrugated paper

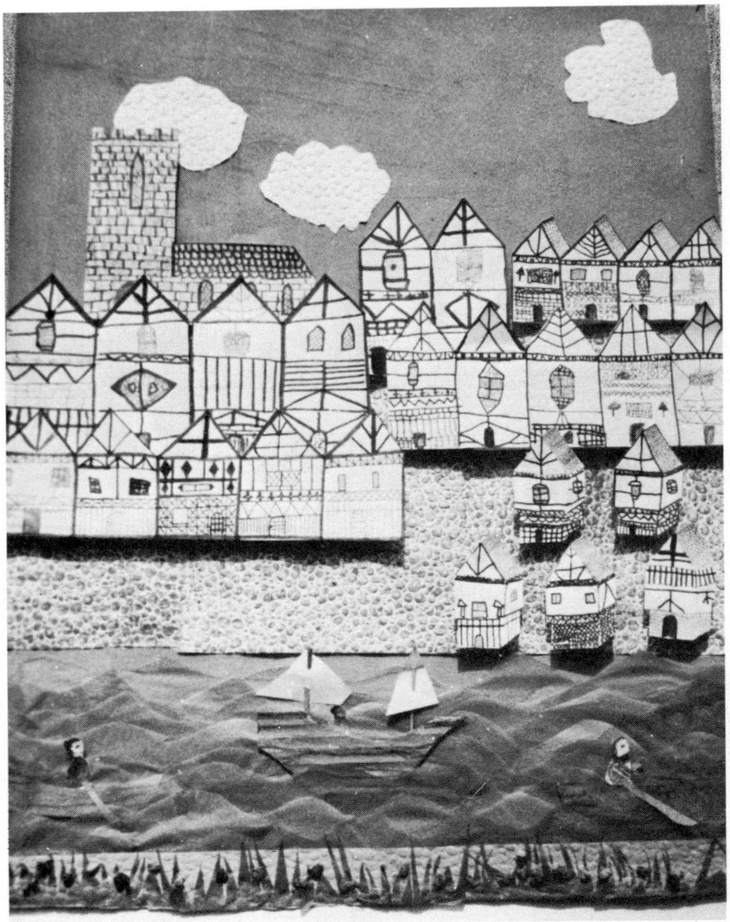

37 Three-dimensional picture using layering and textured papers: children aged 6 and 7

Relief by layering

Relief can be achieved by gluing cardboard shapes one to another so that a stepped progression takes place from the flat surface of the support to the highest levels of the design, see figure 36. The layers may be allowed to overlap so that more intensive shadows result. In figure 37 the rows of houses are supported on blocks of expanded polystyrene and this gives a sense of space and depth to the picture.

Assemblage

Constructed cardboard or paper forms as well as those cut from cartons and packets can be mounted on a backing of hardboard or thick cardboard to make an assemblage. This is, in effect, three-dimensional collage and, like collage, the relationship of the items selected, as well as contrasts of surfaces, colours and so on, must be carefully considered. The items can be painted or, as in figure 38, use can be made of found surfaces, whether coloured, textured, or printed.

38 Assemblage from discarded cartons and packets.

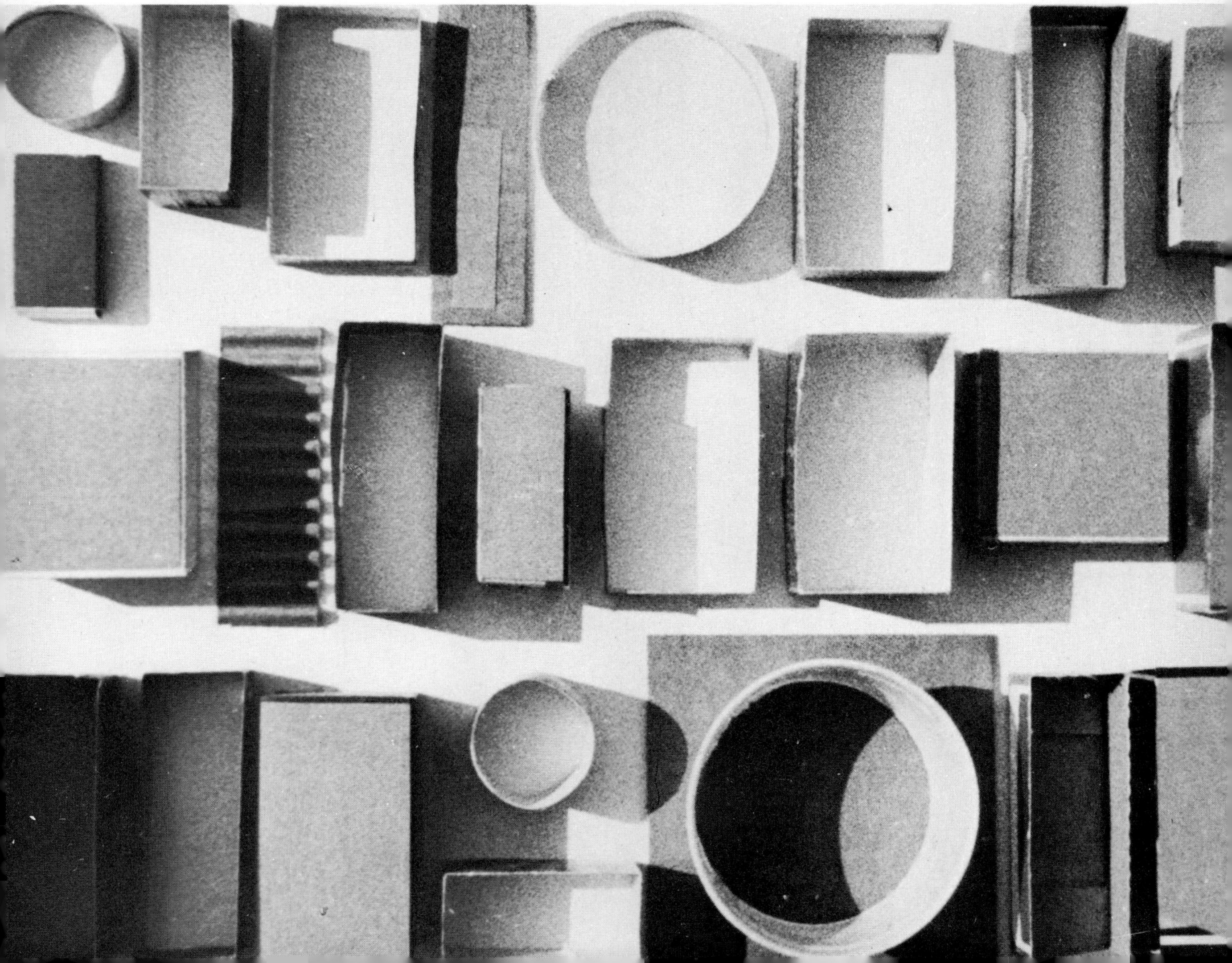

Wood

An important aim of this book is to consider projects and techniques using materials which are readily available to most people. Wood, whether in its natural state or in some processed form is another such material. Wood offers considerable scope for three-dimensional pictures. The ideas explained in this section are adaptable to all levels of ability, just as they can be adapted to involve the use of more unusual materials such as *Perspex (Plexiglas)*, plastics and metals. As with all materials, there is a fundamental requirement to respond to the character and disciplines of the substance being used. Wood will respond well to correct treatment but may well result in complete wastage if used without respect for its various qualities. Similarly, the tools necessary for the cutting and shaping of wood will also demand correct use, for if misused not only will they fail to give the desired result but they could prove dangerous.

Wood is available in various sizes, shapes, types and qualities. The best place to select different types of wood is at a good timber merchant or 'Do-it-yourself' shop which will stock both hardwoods and softwoods as well as plywood and other boards. Wood, like paper and a number of other commodities, has been affected by increasing world demands and in consequence has become quite expensive. Most kinds of wood are priced per foot (305 mm) length. The price is determined by the quality of the wood and the dimensions of its section (thickness and width). It is normally possible to buy oddments and offcuts at much reduced prices. As the price of purchased wood is so expensive it is wise to keep scraps and offcuts for a possible future use and not to overlook the possibility of using waste woods such as packaging material and wooden boxes, as well as 'found' woods such as driftwood, logs and twigs. Local building sites or council tips may provide a source of scrap wood. This can usually be quite easily cleaned up with a smooth plane or surform plane and some glass paper.

Hardwoods are more expensive and difficult to cut but are recommended for work in which the finished surface and edges are important. Although more difficult to saw, hardwoods will not rip and therefore give a neater cut. Softwoods have a tendency to split but are easily sawn, even by children, and are suitable as backing wood for hardboard and other boards. A sheet of three-ply or five-ply plywood makes an ideal support or backing on which to glue or fix wooden shapes. Plywood is made from a number of woods and its construction gives it greater uniformity in strength than, say hardboard, which means that it is unlikely to warp. Also, it has no line of cleavage and therefore will not split when nailed or screwed. Other types of board include block-board, battenboard, chipboard, hardboard and fireboard.

Working in wood may involve large scale designs and when this is so the support, especially if of hardboard, will need backing to prevent it warping and to facilitate framing and hanging. Hardboard is inexpensive and makes an ideal support for assembled designs, that is those which involve gluing shapes to a backing. If the the work is to include nailed or screwed on shapes then obviously the support should be thicker and in such cases plywood and blockboard are recommended. Hardboard supports which are smaller than 380 mm (15 in.) square will normally not require strengthening with wooden battening.

Hardboard is strengthened by constructing a softwood frame support, as illustrated in figure 44. This support is made to the exact dimensions of the sheet of hardboard so that the edges of the hardboard are true with those of the wooden frame. Measure the sheet of hardboard accurately, for its corners may not be exact right-angles. The wooden frame is based on right-angles, so if necessary make the frame slightly smaller than the sheet of hardboard and then plane off the surplus hardboard. 50 mm × 25 mm (2 in. × 1 in.) prepared deal softwood is the most suitable timber to use for the frame.

Two simple ways of making a joint are shown in in figures 39 to 43. The first method illustrated is a butt joint. In this case the battening is cut to the desired lengths, remembering that the top and bottom lengths will be identical to the length of the hardboard, whereas the side lengths will be equivalent to the width of the hardboard minus two widths of the battening wood. Each corner is made in the way illustrated in figure 39. Where the two pieces of wood meet they are simply glued with *Evo-stick, Uhu, Bostik* or another suitable wood glue and screwed or pinned (nailed) across the joint to give added support and to hold the pieces of wood in place whilst the glue is drying. Further strength can be given to a butt joint by cutting a triangle of hardboard and gluing and pinning this across the angle of the joint, as shown in figure 40. 20 mm (¾ in.) panel pins should be used for this.

An alternative method is to make a half-joint at each corner. This is slightly more difficult but will produce a more rigid framework support for the hardboard. For this method cut the lengths of timber to correspond to the width and length of the sheet of hardboard. The joint at each corner of the frame is then made as illustrated in figure 41. Measure in from each end of each length of the wood to a point which is exactly equivalent to the width of the wood and then make a cut with a tenon saw through half the thickness. Cut in from half way across the end section of the wood to meet the first cut so that a small block of wood is removed giving a stepped appearance to the end of each of the lengths of wood. Make sure that correspondingly opposite cuts are made in the top and bottom lengths to those of the side pieces, so that they interlock. These joints can be pinned and glued, as illustrated in figure 42, and again further strengthened with triangular pieces of hardboard, as shown in figure 43.

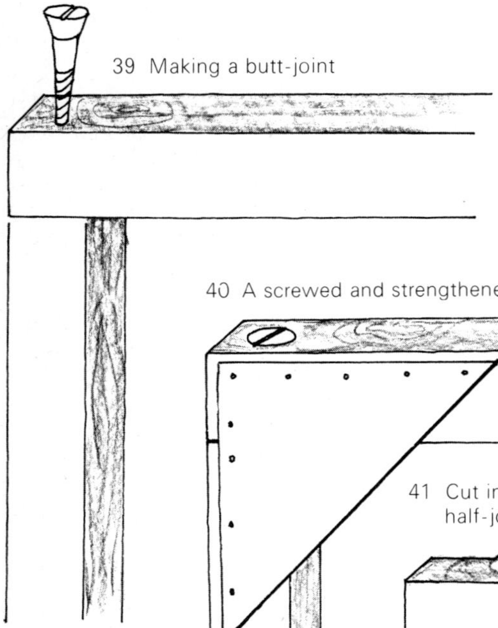

39 Making a butt-joint

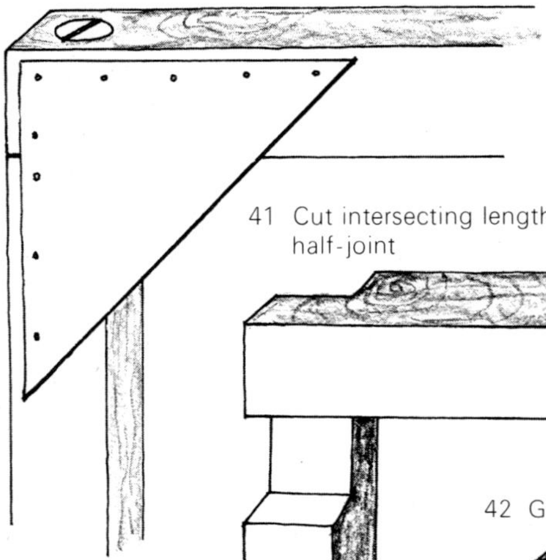

40 A screwed and strengthened butt-joint

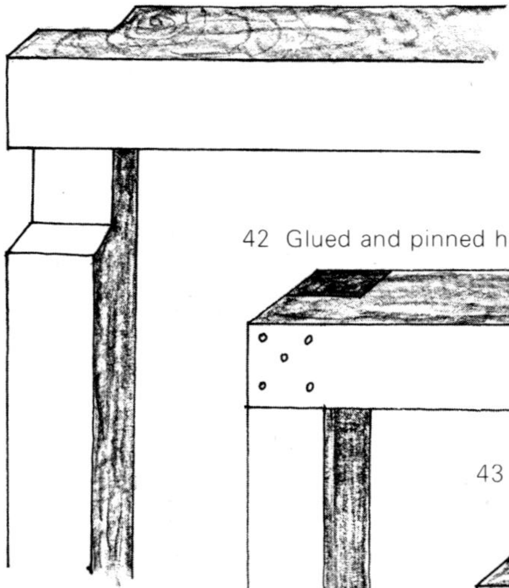

41 Cut intersecting lengths of wood to make a half-joint

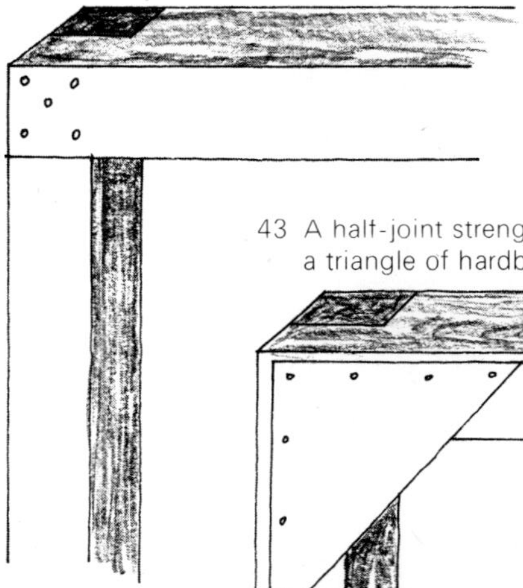

42 Glued and pinned half-joint

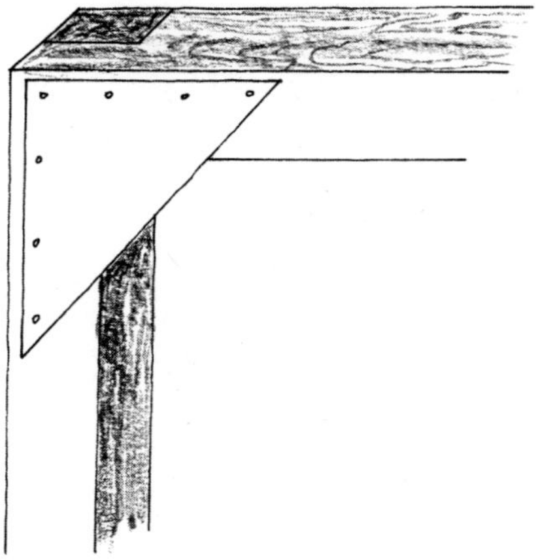

43 A half-joint strengthened with a triangle of hardboard

When the wooden framework has been constructed by butt-jointing or half-jointing each corner, the sheet of hardboard can be glued on to it, again with *Evo-stick* or another impact adhesive or wood glue. Allow this to dry before trimming off any surplus, or sizing or preparing the board. It may be necessary to apply some sort of weight to the hardboard to hold it in place whilst the glue dries. Large panels may need additional cross-pieces, as shown in figure 44.

The support for a three-dimensional picture using wood, whether it be of backed hardboard or blockboard or plywood, may need preparing in some way before beginning to attach shapes to form the picture. This will depend entirely on what sort of work is envisaged. If, for example, the whole area is to be covered by gluing on shapes, then it is going to be unnecessary to size, paint or varnish the support beforehand.

As with other types of work it is advisable to arrange the component parts of the picture in place before any are firmly secured. This will enable alterations to be made to the design and the possibility of experimenting with parts in different places. Wooden shapes can be painted with emulsion, gloss or enamel paint as well as acrylic and PVA paints and *Reeves Craft Paint*. Wood can also be varnished with a suitable matt or gloss varnish, such as *Ronseal* hardglaze polyurethane wood seal, or simply left in its natural state, exploiting variations of texture, grain and natural contrasts in colouring. When completed, the picture can be framed by attaching lengths of battening to the wooden surround of the hardboard or on to the thickness of the plywood or blockboard support. Battening used for this purpose should normally be about twice as wide as the width of the support so as to give the effect of enclosing the picture. Battening can be mitred, that is cut at an angle of 45 degrees, by using a tenon saw and mitre box, or with a machine. Otherwise lengths of wood used for this purpose may be butt-jointed as already described, making the top and bottom lengths equal to the size of the picture and the side lengths long enough to overlap on to these and so disquise the joint. Of course, other more elaborate frames may be fitted but always bear in mind that the frame is simply there to finish the work, to enhance it, but never to detract from it. A mitred length of battening is shown attached to the left-hand side of a backed hardboard support in figure 44.

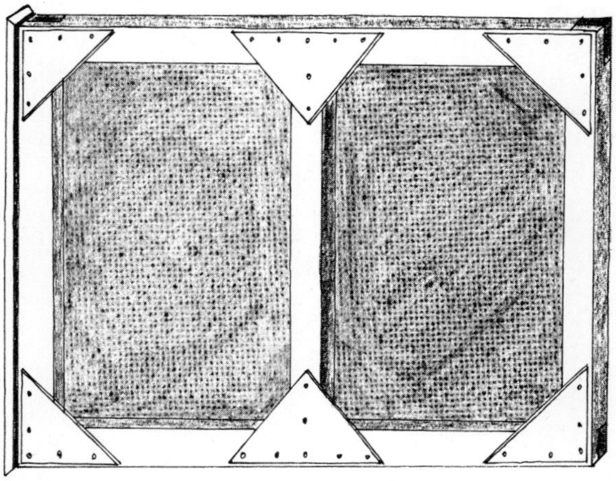

44 A backed hardboard support

Using wood will necessitate certain additional equipment. Basic tools will be a tenon saw, a hammer, a chisel and a rasp. Holes can be drilled with a brace and bit, a hand drill or an electric drill. Final smoothing and polishing is done with a file and glass paper. The availability of a vice and a workbench is an obvious advantage. The *Eclipse* 66 general purpose saw is extremely useful as it cuts wood, metal, plastics and fibreboard. A tenon saw will suit the cutting of blocks and strips of thin wood whilst larger boards can be cut with a hand saw. Fretsaws and coping saws are useful for cutting shapes from hardboard or thin plywood. Additional tools can include a smooth plane or surform plane, pliers, a nail punch, a mallet, screwdrivers and clamps. Electrical equipment can be dangerous and should not be operated by the inexperienced except under close supervision.

Layers

Shapes cut from various types of board and plywood can be used to build up relief in a series of layers. In designing such pictures one can use contrasts in size and shape, variations in colour, different types of wood and variations in relief. The example illustrated in figure 45 was constructed from layers of hardboard and block-board glued to a hardboard support. The whole surface was painted with emulsion paint, thus using the shadows as an important part of the design. This design incorporates drilled wood and dowelling with the layered blocks. Similar work could take the form of a silhouette cut with a fretsaw from board and decorated by gluing on strips and layers of wood, perhaps brush or spray painted.

Blocks

Three-dimensional pictures can be assembled by using blocks of wood and various ideas using this technique are illustrated in figures 46 to 52. Again, make use of contrasts in size and thickness as well as different types of wood. The blocks of wood can be combined with paper shapes, figure 49, or painted shapes, figure 50. Round blocks cut from dowelling or a broom-handle can be used, as in figure 51, which combines these with textured and smooth layers of hard-board and corks. The butterfly illustrated in figure 52 was made from the sawn sections of a log, the antennae of this insect being made from wood shavings.

45 Designing with layers of wood

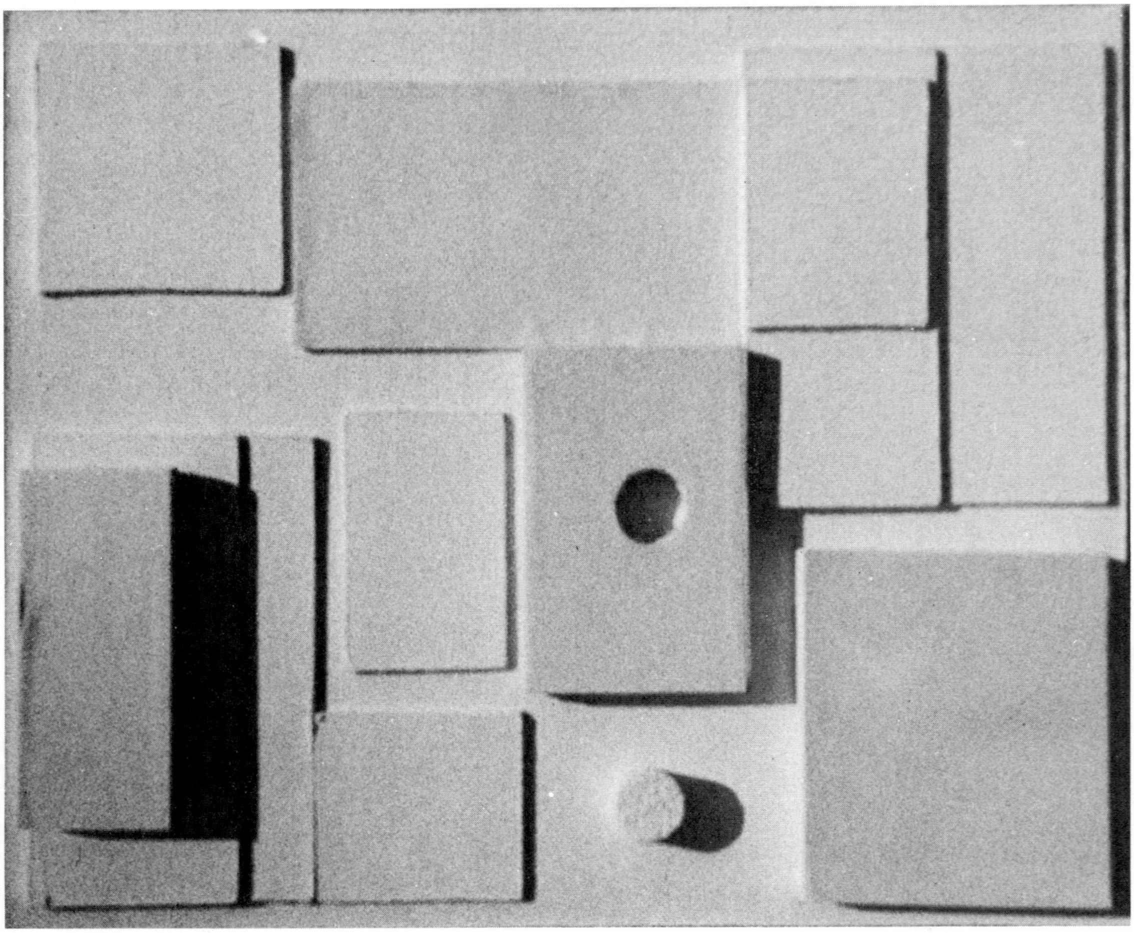

46 Sergio de Camergo, *Large split white relief*: split lime wood cylinders on a plywood backing. The Tate Gallery, London

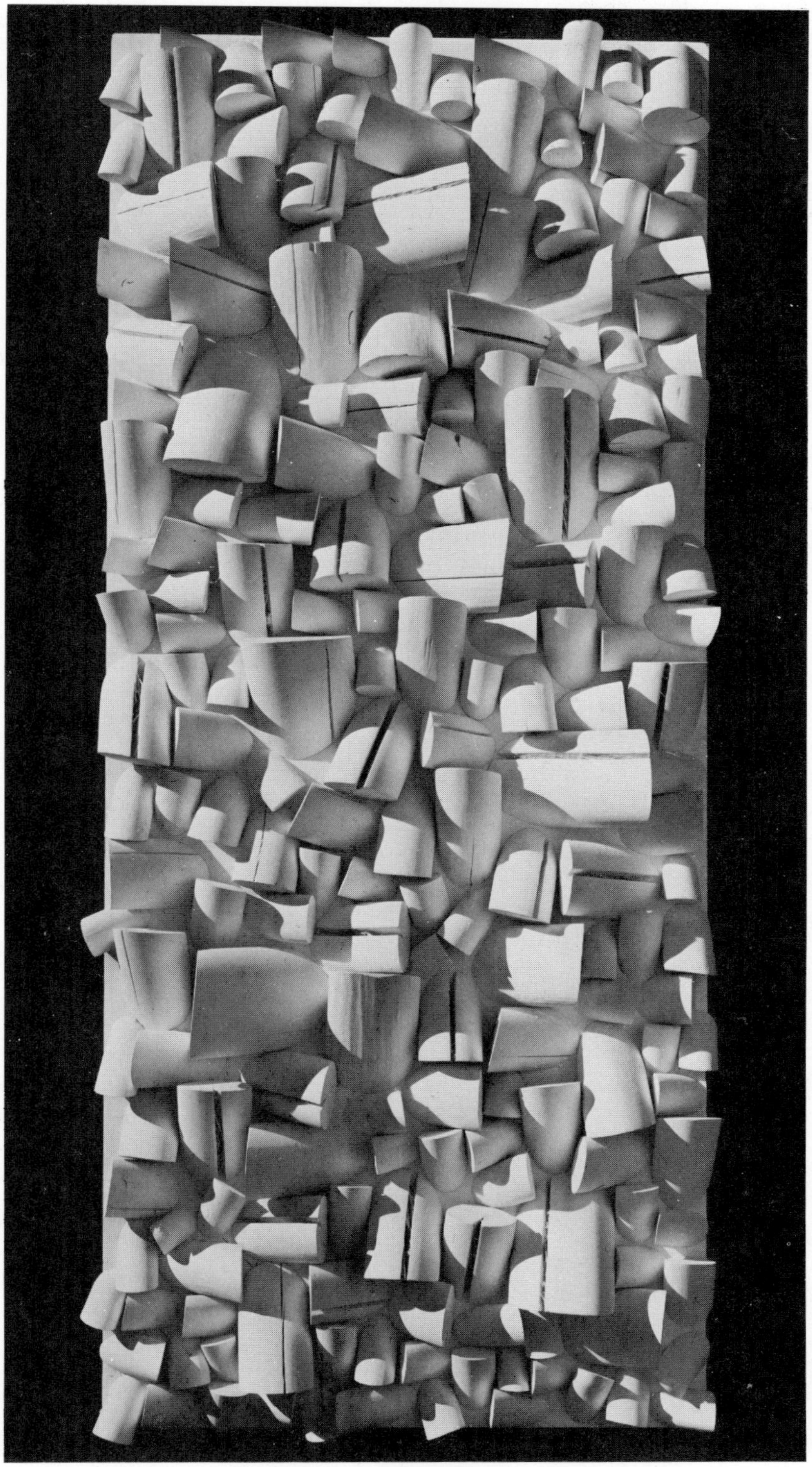

47 Shaped blocks of softwood

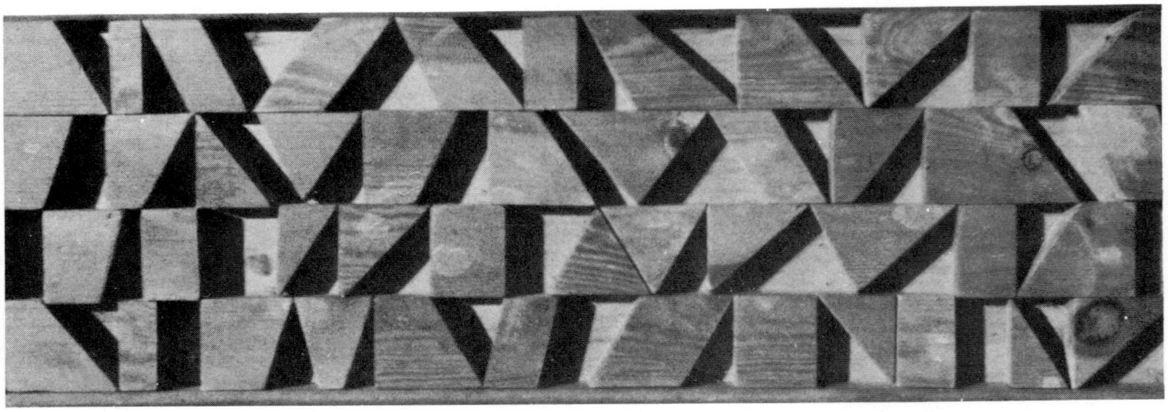

48 Blocks cut from various types of wood

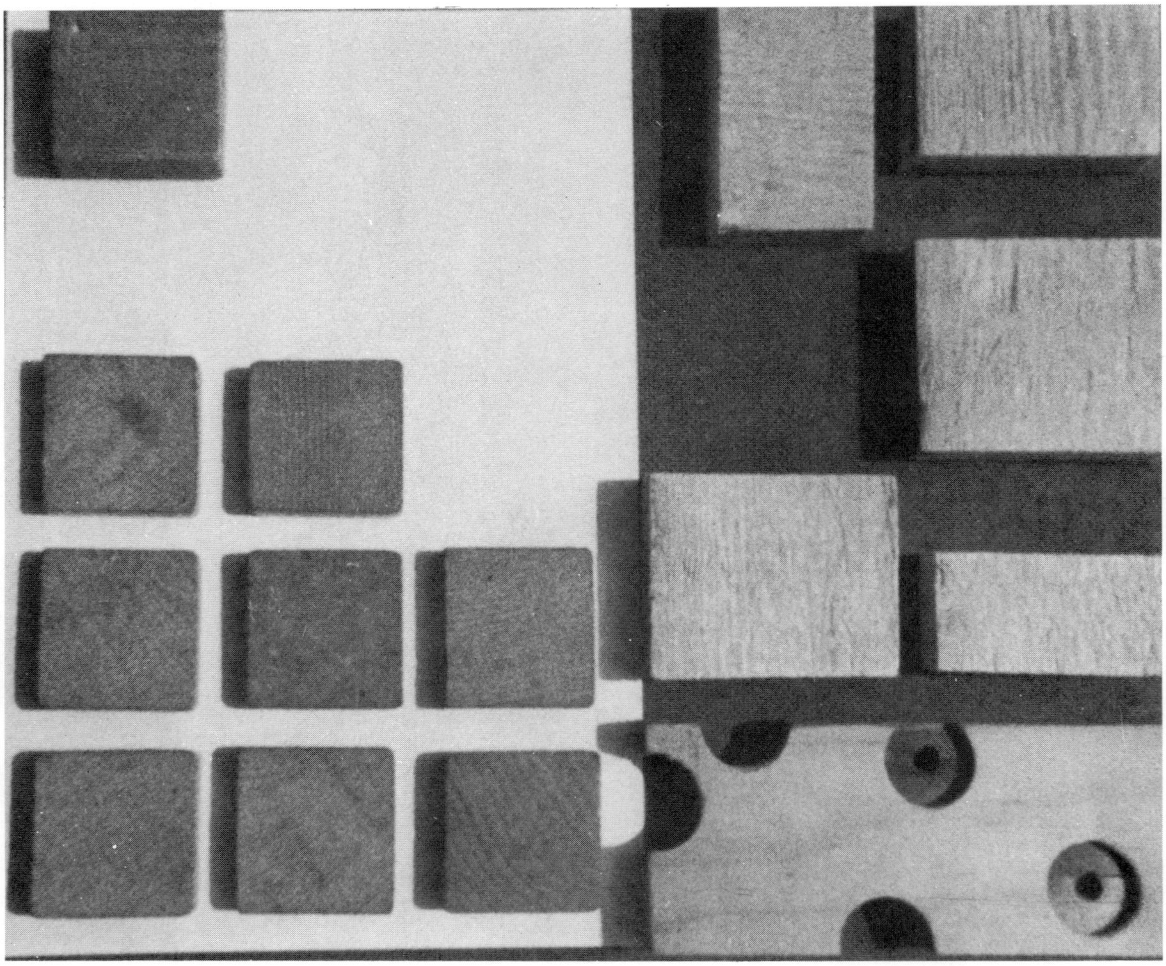

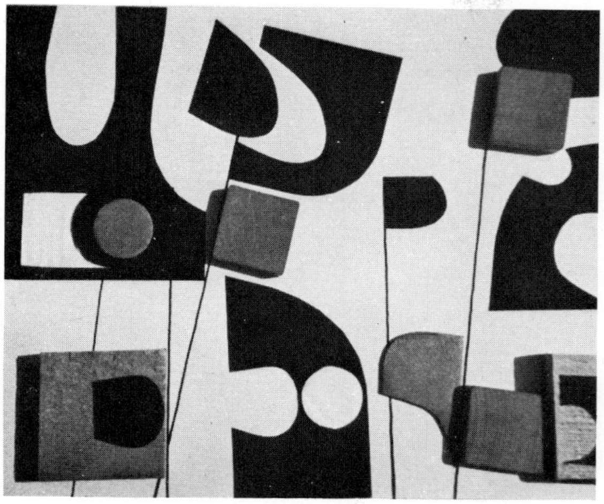

49 Combining blocks of wood with shapes cut from paper and cardboard

50 Blocks and painted shapes

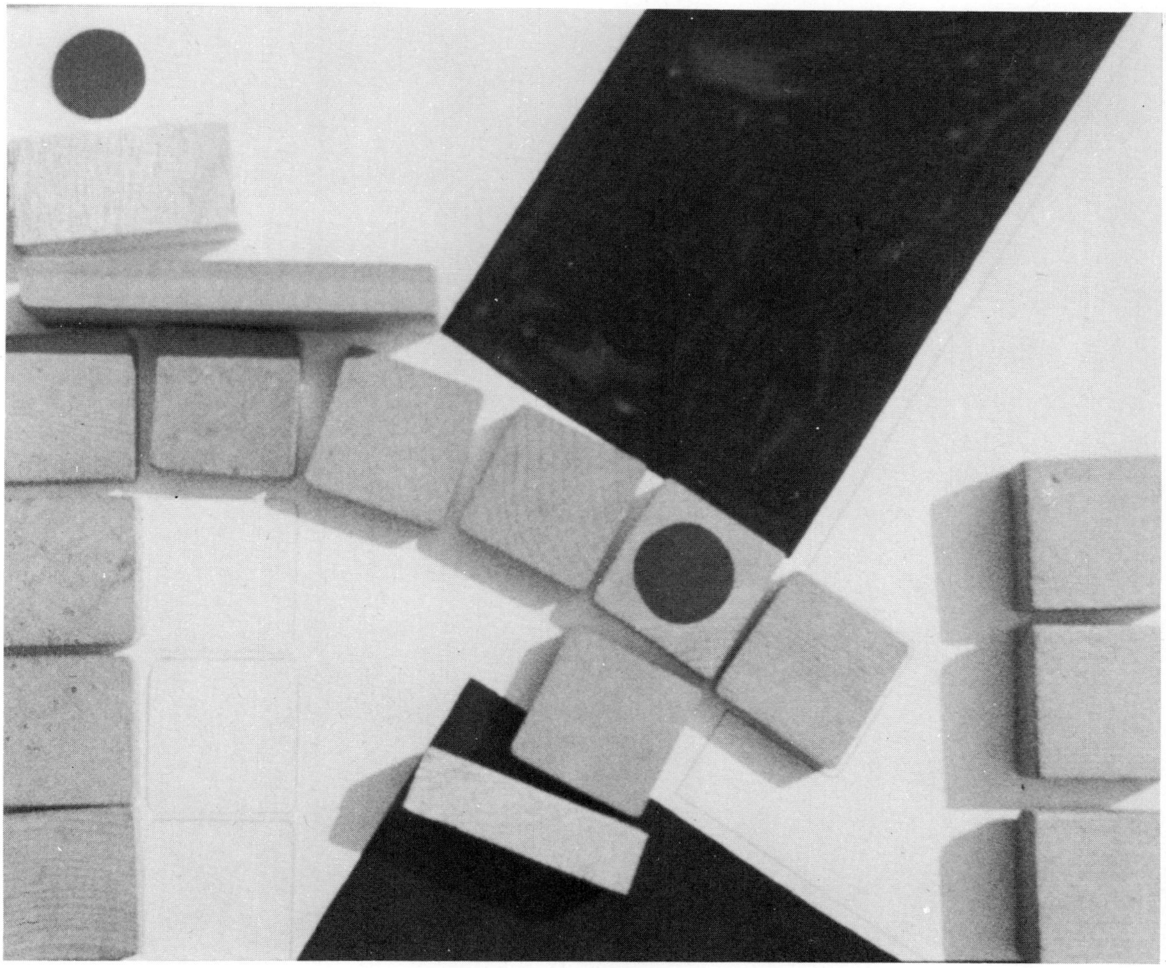

51 Dowelling

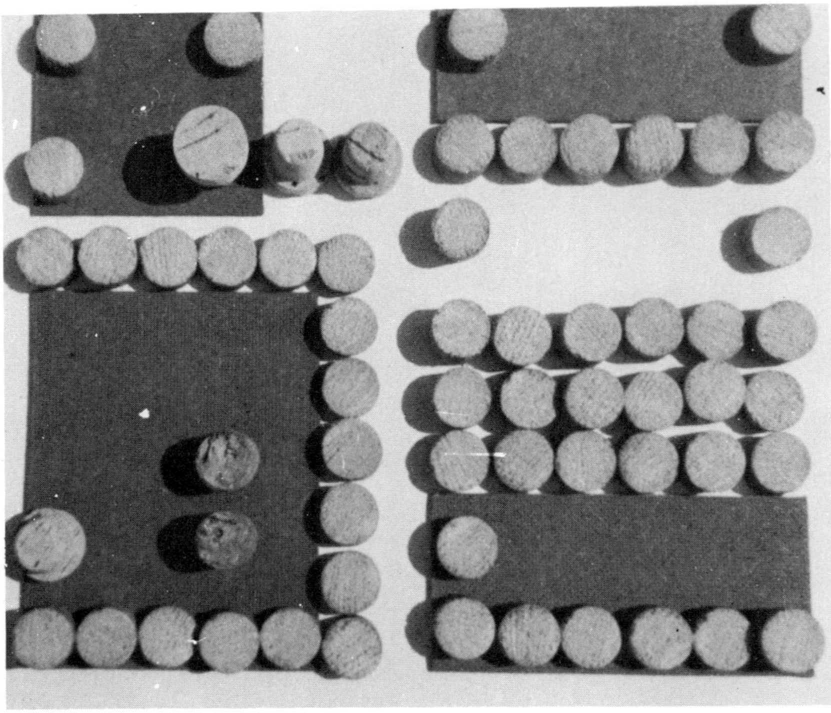

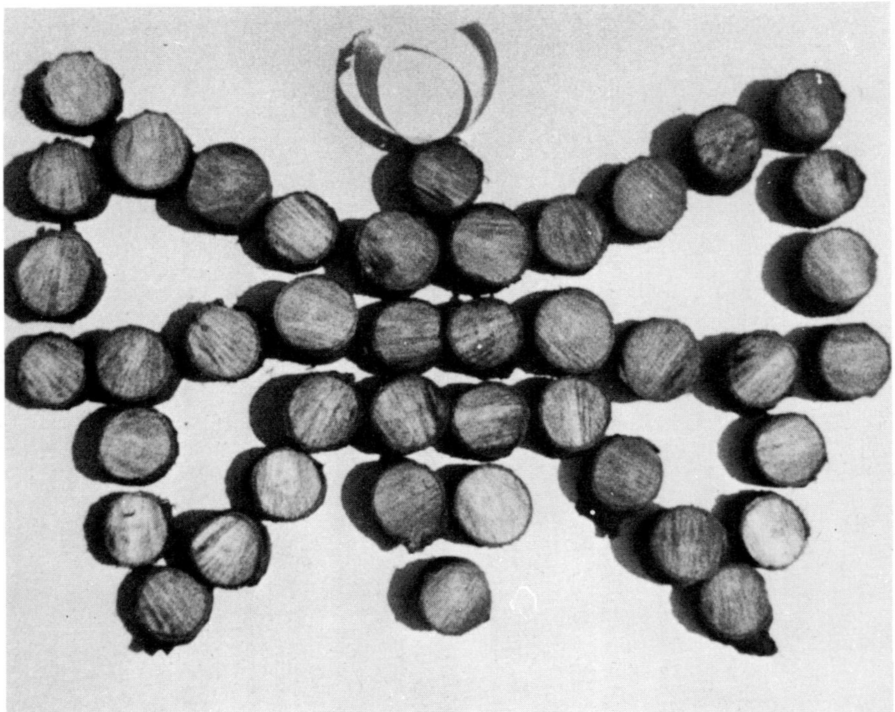

52 Sawn logwood and shavings

53 Incorporating painted strips of wood

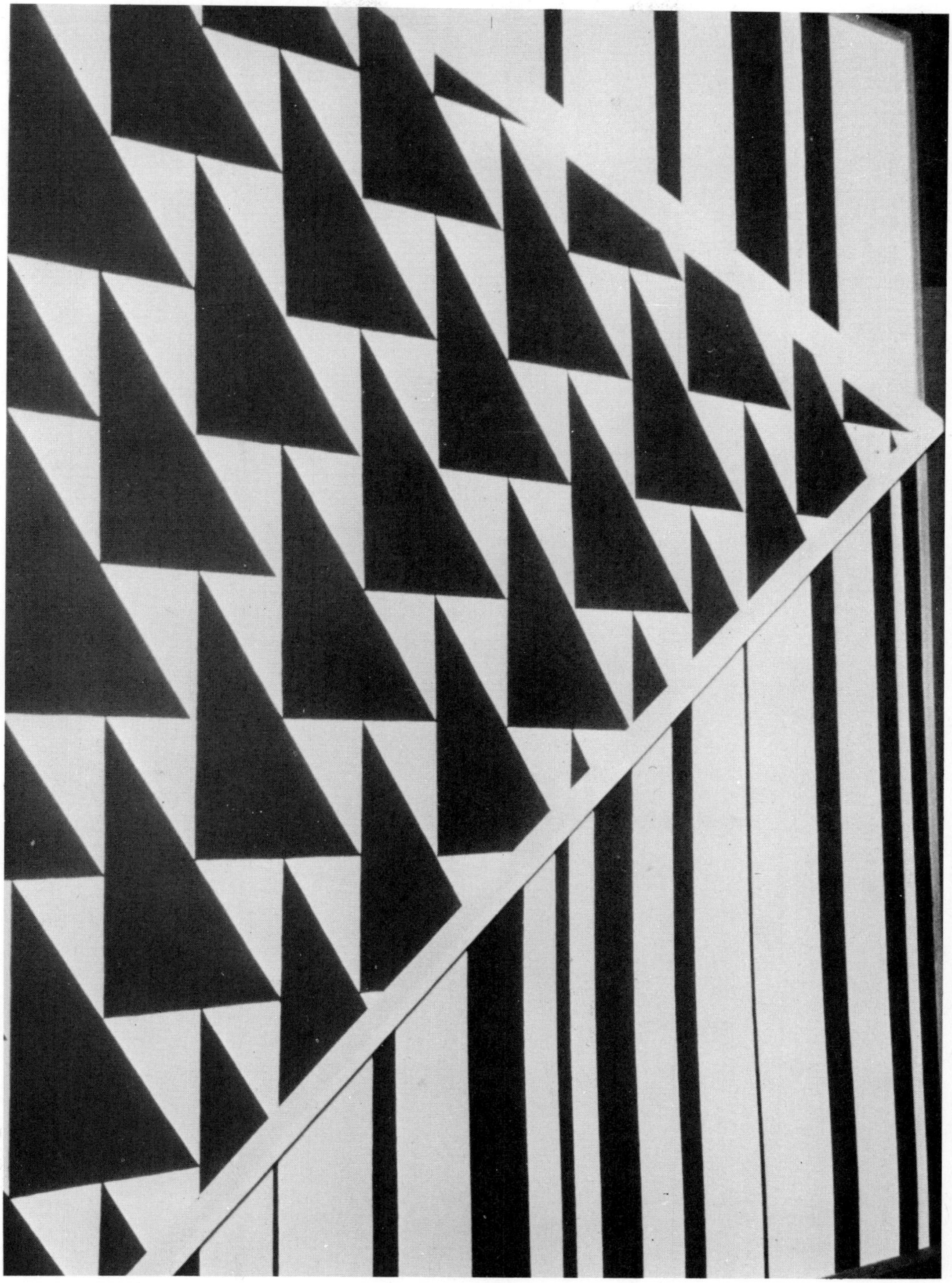

Strips

Interesting results are possible by introducing strips of wood into a painting. This may be particularly so with abstract designs which may wish to exploit the third-dimension as a contrast to the flat painted surface. In figure 53, for example, painted strips of wood have been used to make a large triangular shape running across the painting which is in contrast to the painted triangles and strips. In this example the strips also have an illusionary effect, seeming to make the central, triangular area protrude from the rest of the painting. Painted strips have also been used in figure 54.

Picture-building with strips of wood is a good way of employing offcuts which would otherwise seem to have no use. Children enjoy making pictures from offcut strips and blocks; they can select the size they require and there is no need for them to have to use a saw or any other equipment as the strips are simply glued in place on a strong cardboard or hardboard backing. In fact PVA adhesive, which was recommended for paper and cardboard, will readily stick thin blocks of wood. See figure 55.

54 Using painted strips of wood

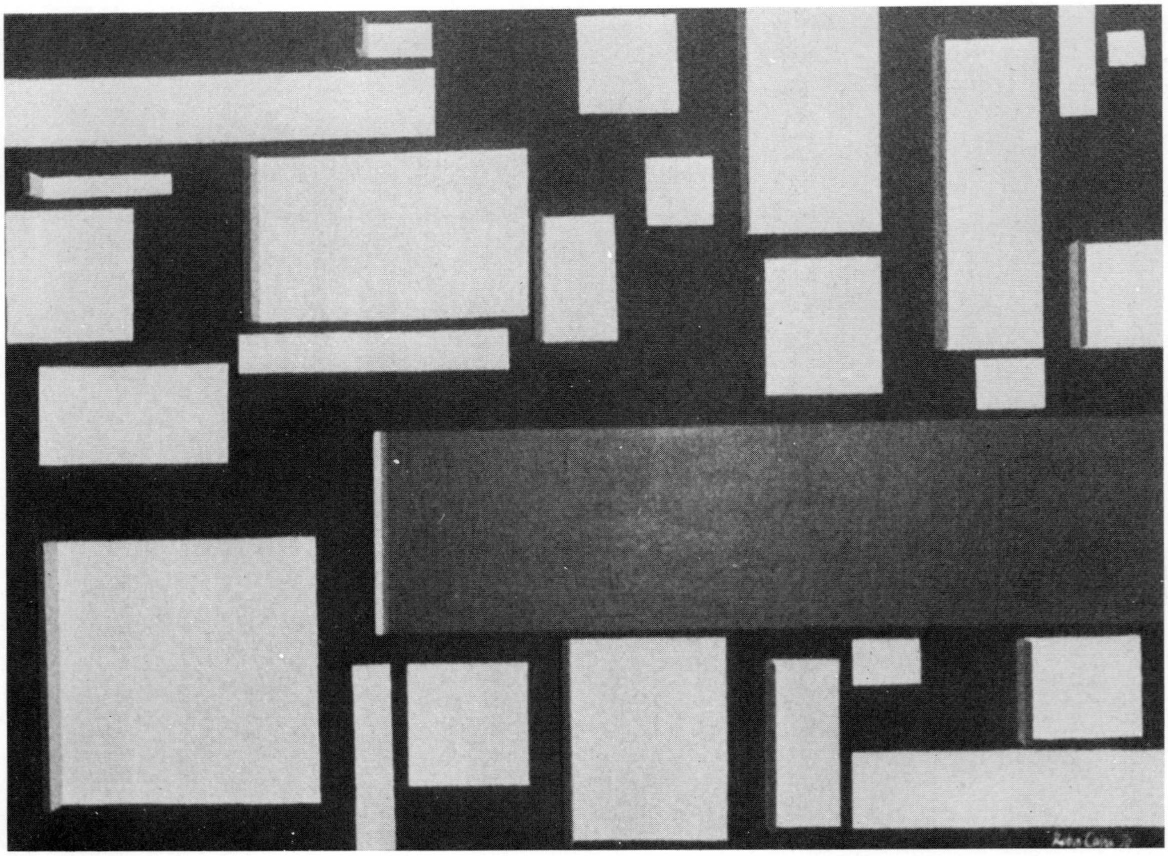

Of course, materials and techniques can be combined. In figure 56 blocks and strips of wood as well as wood shavings and paper have been used.

Balsa wood is another useful material. It is easily cut with a craft knife and thin strips can in fact be cut with scissors, making it suitable for use by quite young children. Balsa cement, or more economically PVA adhesive, is used to stick blocks and strips to a paper, cardboard or hardboard support. In figure 57 thin strips of balsa have been used, in some places being built up to produce contrasting, stronger shadows. In figure 58 the figure and wheels were made from thin aluminium modelling wire.

55 Picture-building with wooden strips

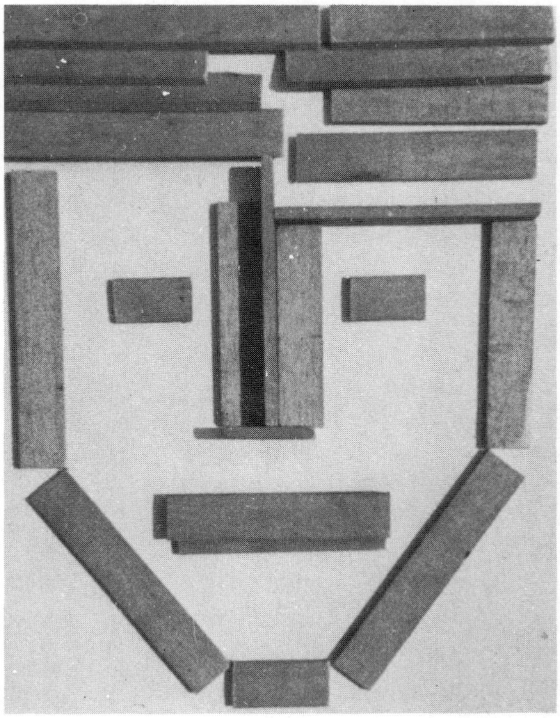

56 Combining various shapes and materials

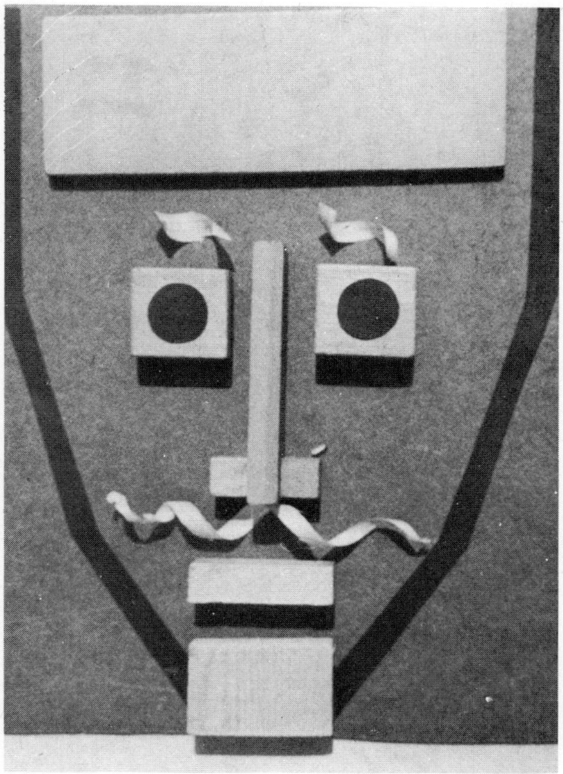

Waste wood

The possibility of using waste wood has been mentioned; picture-making with scraps and offcuts of wood particularly suits young children who seem to find more potential and expressiveness in these materials than do most adults. The various oddments need securing to a backing, using glues and supports previously recommended.

Various types of waste have been used in figure 59; matchsticks, twigs, bark and sawdust, as well as paper and crushed egg shells. Twigs and bark have also been used for figure 62, whilst the following illustration was made from coloured sawdust, twigs and wood shavings.

57 Balsa wood design

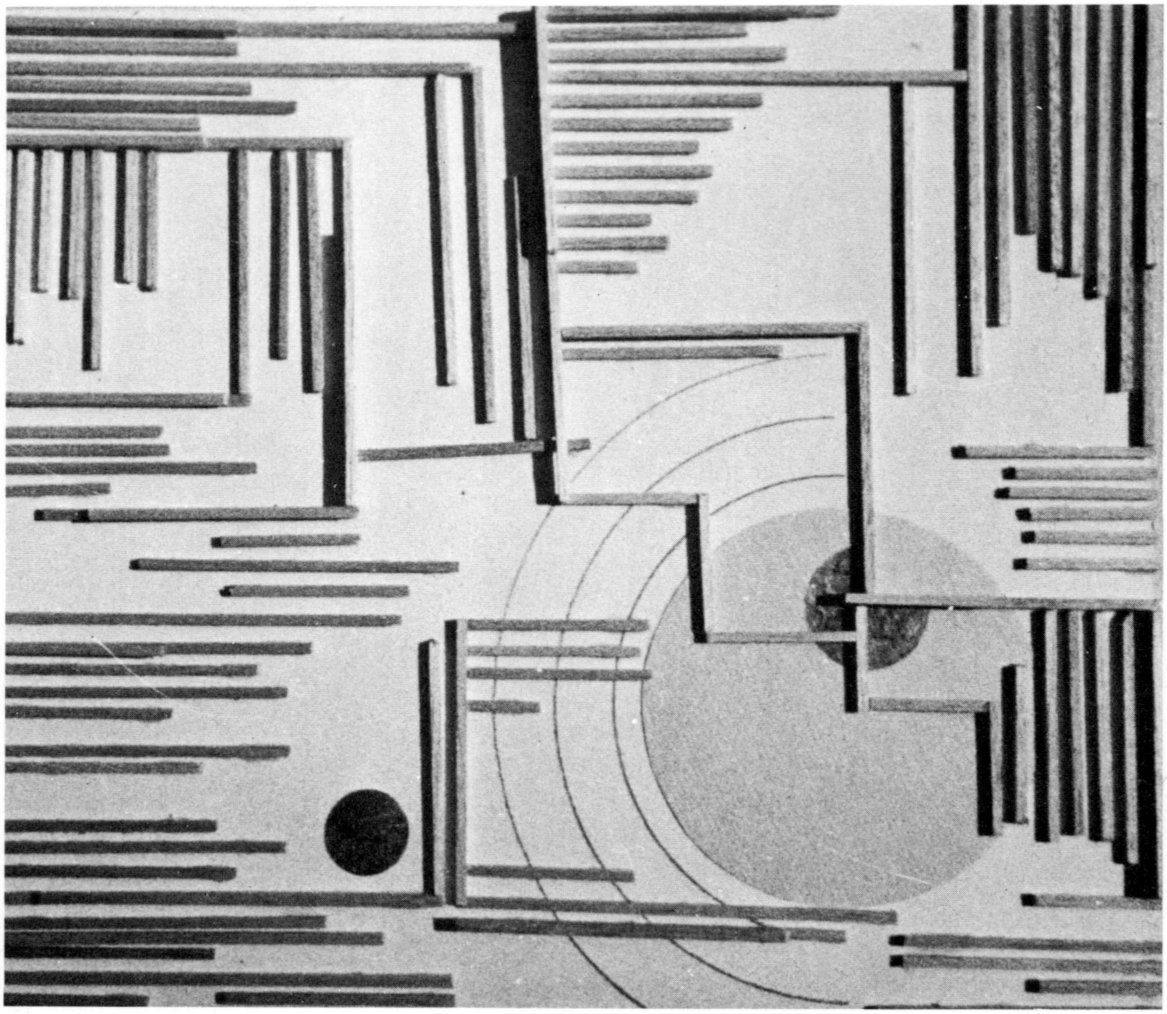

58 Balsa wood design: girl aged 8

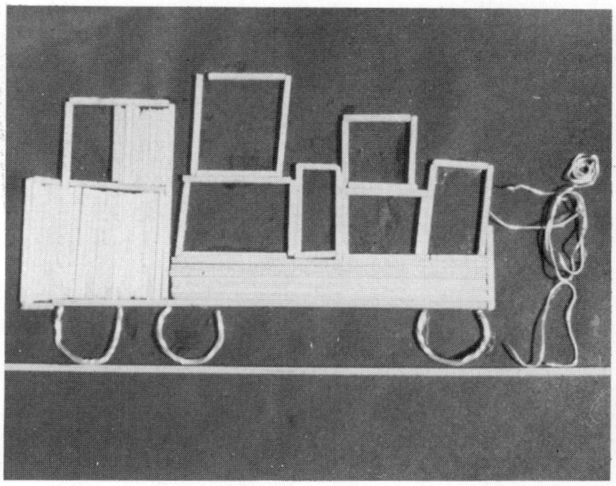

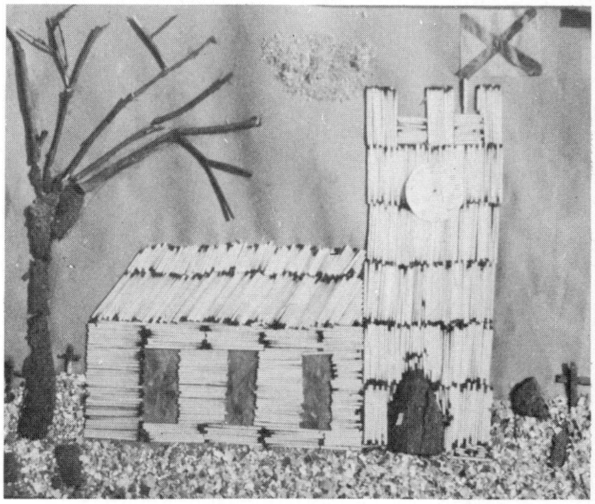

59 Match sticks and other materials: girl aged 8

60 Using wooden offcuts: boy aged 6

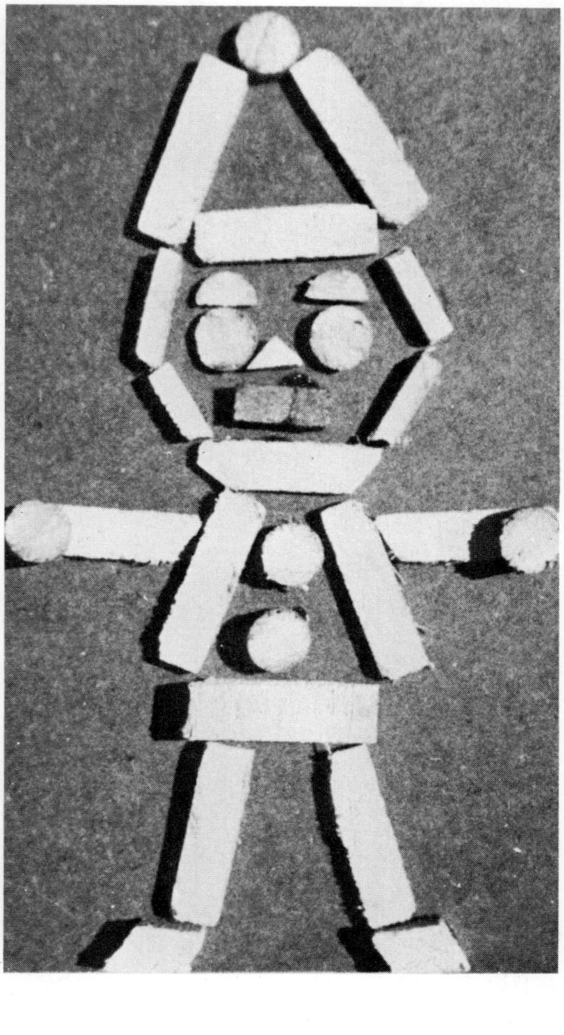

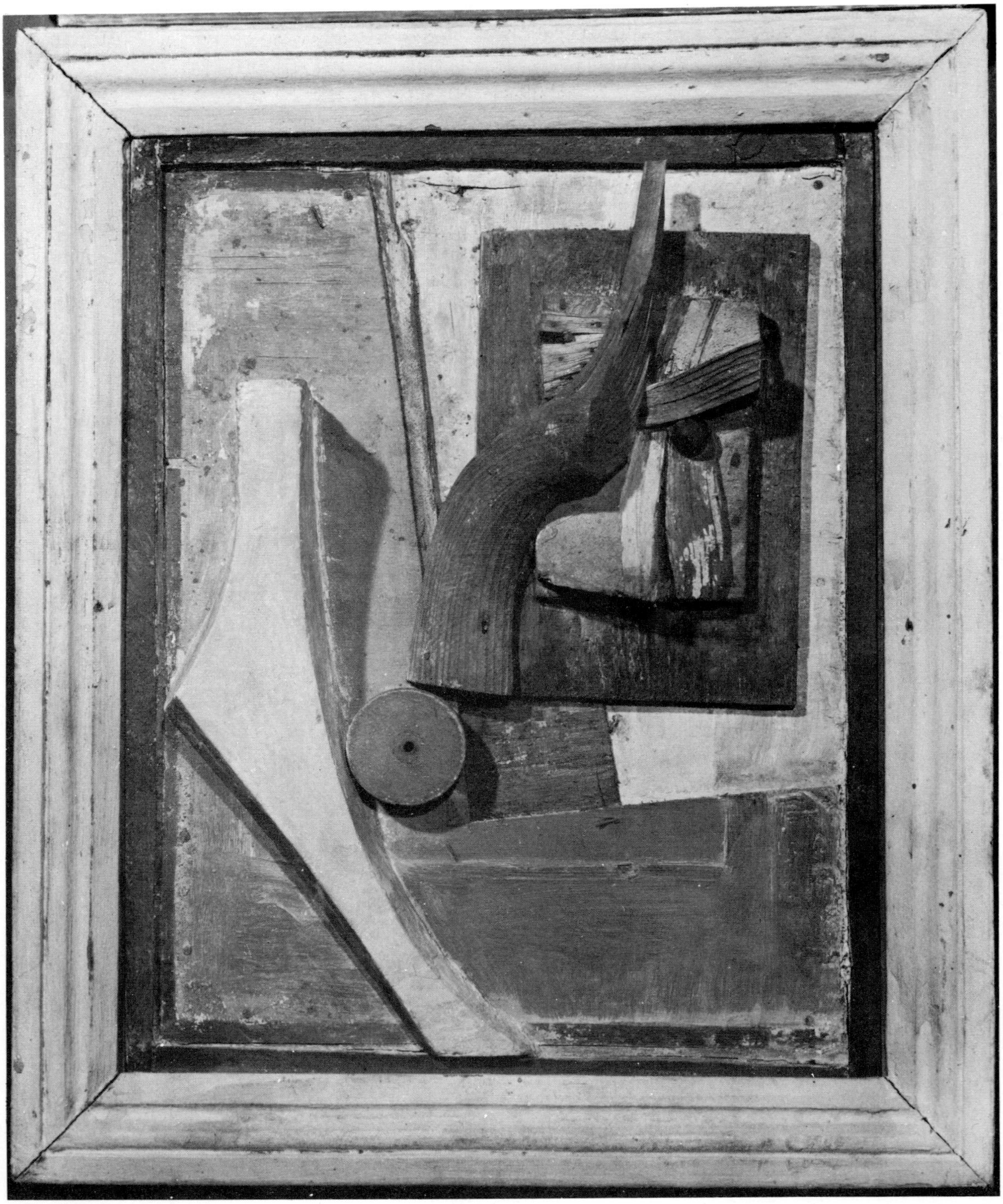

61 Kurt Schwitters, *Many Angles*.
The Tate Gallery, London

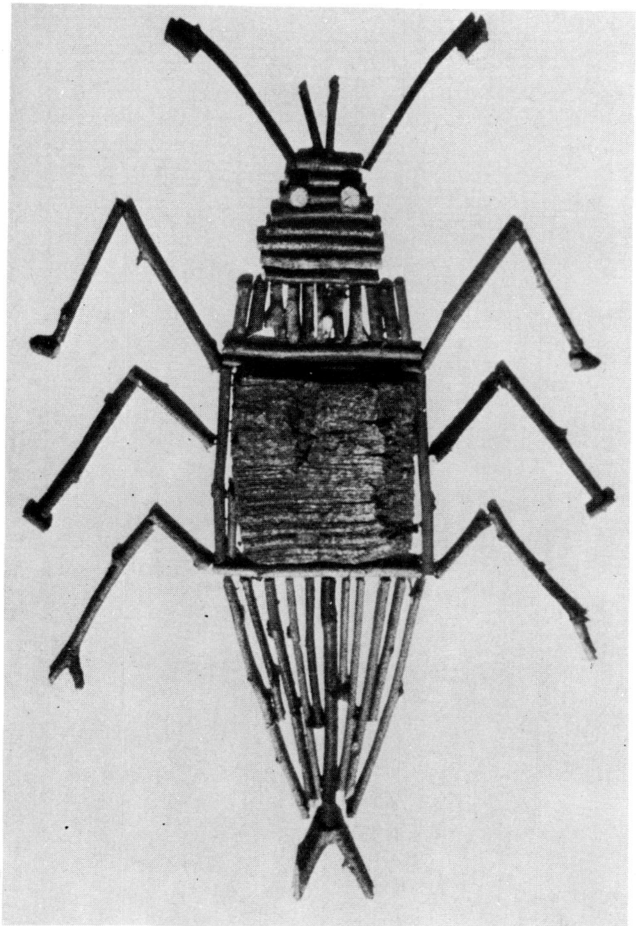

62 Twigs and bark

63 Wood shavings, sawdust and twigs: girl aged 8

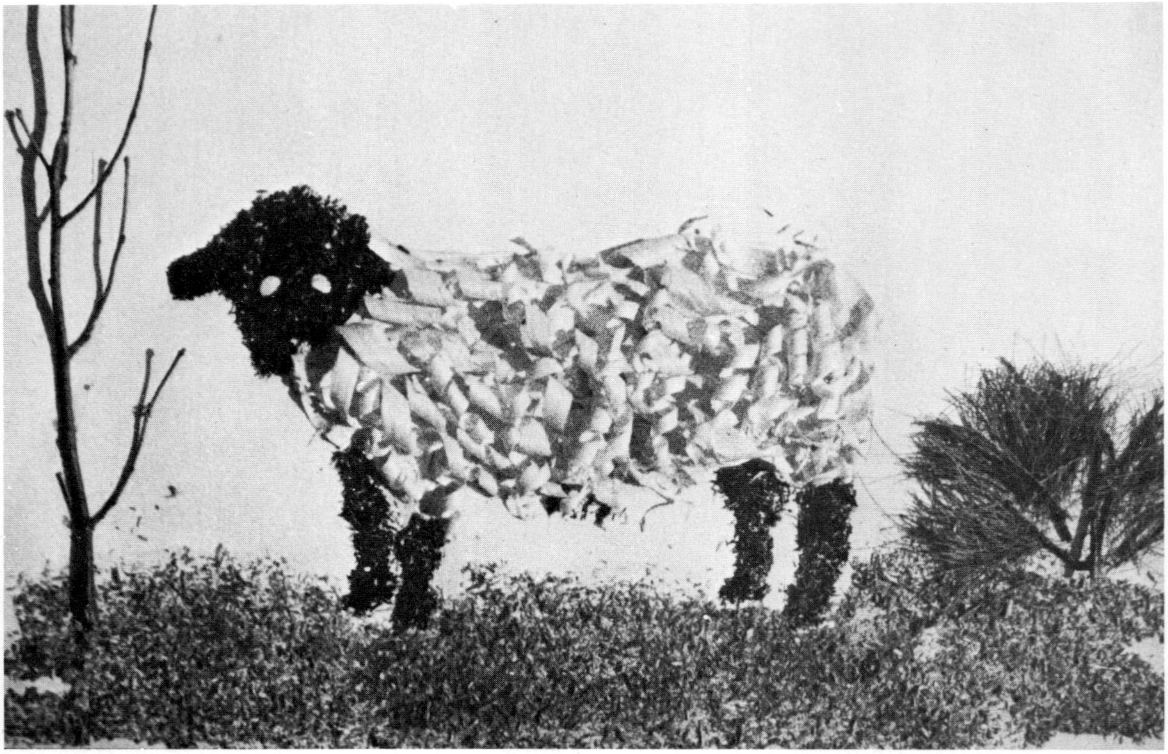

Nails

Three-dimensional pictures can be made by nailing or screwing wooden shapes to a backing of plywood or blockboard. The use of nails or screws can look very obvious as opposed to the 'hidden' method of fixing when glue is used. The round and oval shapes of the heads of the nails should be exploited as part of the design, the nails therefore becoming integrated and unobtrusive—small wire nails 25 mm (1 in.) are usually the most suitable for joining parts of a simple construction, though the length and type of nails will need to relate to the thickness and types of wood being used.

Nails and screws can also serve a decorative purpose, as in figure 64. In this example the flat heads of felt nails have been glued to the support so that the points protrude. Variations in sizes and types of nails and driving them in at different angles to create movement and direction are factors which can be considered. Pictures can be designed entirely of nails or by combining nails with thread. Aluminium alloy nails, panel pins, veneer pins, clasp nails, clout nails, tacks, brass chair nails, and wire staples are among useful types. Wood screws are available in three basic types: countersunk, roundhead and oval head.

64 Using nails

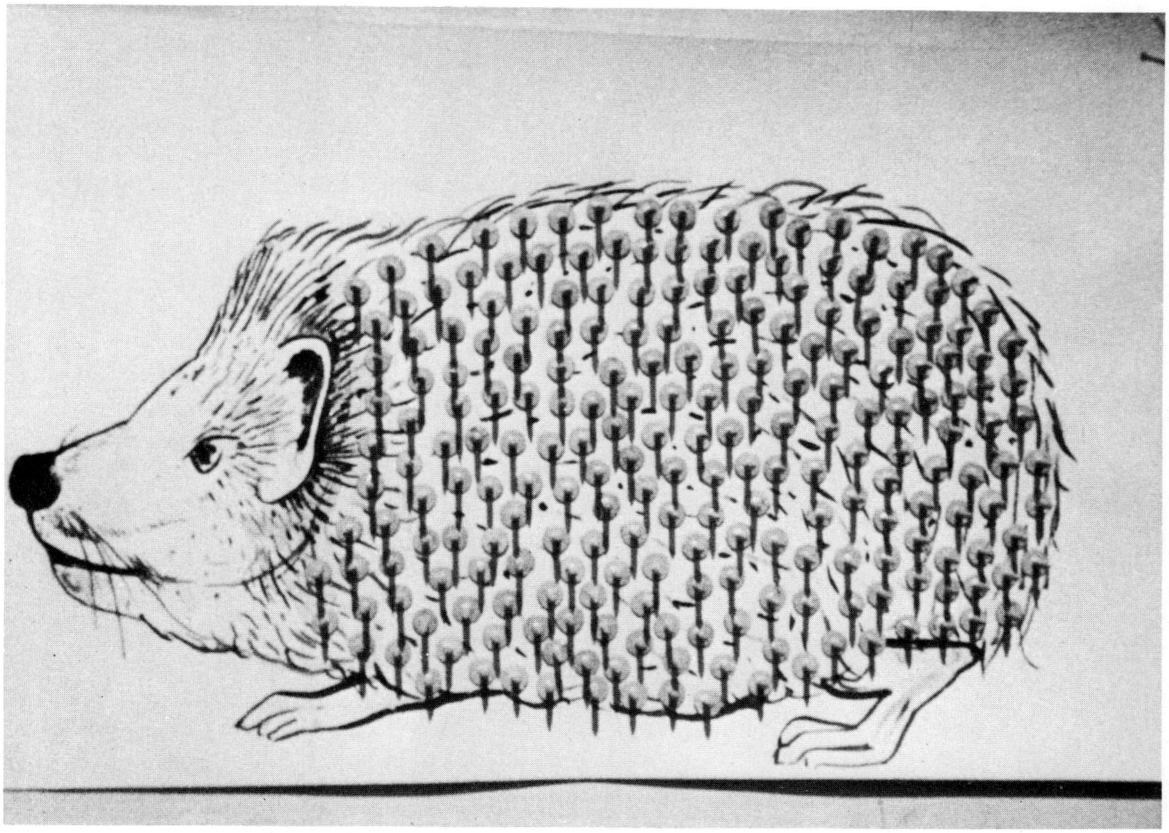

Expanded Polystyrene

Expanded polystyrene is another material which is inexpensive and readily available and which is clean and easy to use. It is a versatile material which is easily cut and shaped and thus suitable for a wide range of work at all age levels.

Expanded polystyrene is now widely used as packaging material, especially for large household goods and appliances, and specially shaped blocks which have been used for this purpose make an exciting source of material for creative work. It may be possible to obtain unwanted blocks of this type from a shop which sells electrical appliances. Polystyrene tiles can be obtained from builders' merchants and 'Do-it-yourself' shops, whilst spheres, cubes and other interesting shapes are available from various art suppliers and manufacturers (see suppliers list). Ceiling tiles are available in different sizes and thicknesses and some shops stock patterned tiles. Tiles measuring 70 mm (2 ft) square are obtainable and these make ideal supports for applied work. Scraps and offcuts are useful, as always.

Tiles may be cut with a sharp craft knife or safety razor blade. If straight edges are required then use the knife against a metal ruler. Duplicate shapes can be made by using a cardboard shape as a template around which to cut. Expanded polystyrene has an open cellular structure which means that it cannot be carved with a knife or cut with scissors, as any form of cutting which depends on pressure merely breaks down the cells and causes the substance to crumble. Instead, the only other method of cutting or shaping the polystyrene is to apply heat to it. Expanded polystyrene has the characteristic of other thermoplastics of softening when heated and hardening quickly if allowed to cool. Tiles and blocks may therefore be cut with a heated piece of wire, a battery operated hot-wire cutter or an electric hot-wire cutter. Battery operated cutters are available from some hard-ware stores or electrical appliance shops. It is quite easy to make your own cutter by simply using a length of bent wire, by mounting the wire in a wooden handle, or, for detail work, by embedding a needle into a cork. The end of the wire or needle can then be heated in a candle flame, as illustrated in figure 65. Polystyrene can also be scorched and burnt by holding it over a candle flame or bunsen burner. The burning and heating of polystyrene is, of course, possibly dangerous, not only as a fire risk but also due to the fact that hot polystyrene gives off toxic fumes. The process must therefore be carried out in a well ventilated room and in supervised conditions which do not constitute a potential fire risk or contravene fire regulations.

There are several methods of joining expanded polystyrene shapes. Heated shapes will attach to each other simply by applying pressure. The use of solvents such as nail varnish and cellulose paints will also enable shapes to be joined by pressure. However, possibly the best and certainly the most reliable methods are by pinning the shapes together with steel pins or by gluing them. Heavy-duty wallpaper paste can be used for joining thin polystyrene shapes and layers whilst other suitable adhesives include PVA, *Marvin Medium*, and *Elmer's glue*. Other glues may be solvent and if so will melt the surface of the polystyrene. Before using an adhesive other than those recommended it may therefore be advisable to make a test on some small scraps or offcuts. Most glues take longer to dry when used on the polystyrene surface and glued shapes may need holding in place with pins to prevent them slipping. The pins can be removed when the glue has dried.

Thin polystyrene tiles make useful supports and shapes can also be glued to a backing of paper, cardboard, hardboard or plywood.

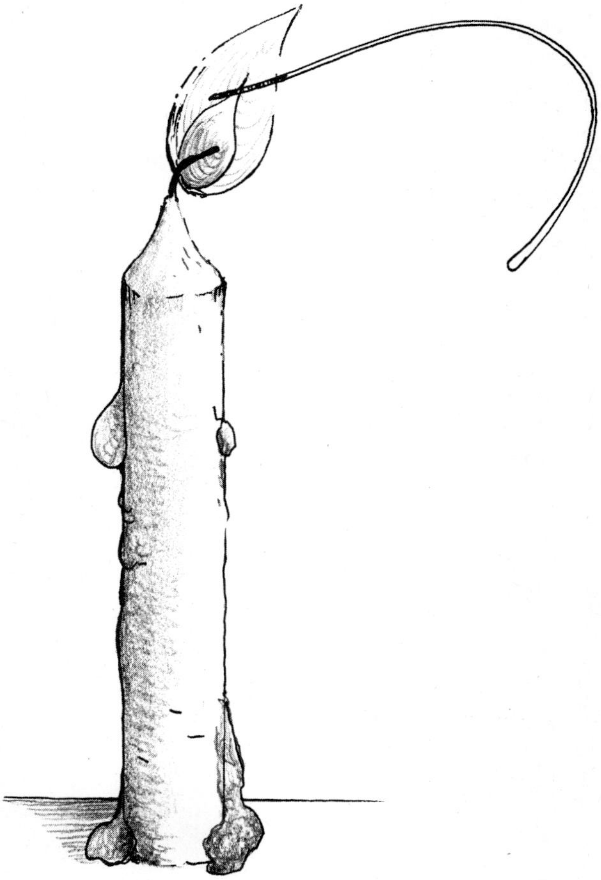

65 Heating a bent piece of wire through a candle flame. The heated wire will easily cut polystyrene.

Extended and silhouette designs from a polystyrene tile

Ceiling tiles are useful for design exercises and many of the ideas which can be achieved in paper or cardboard can equally well be applied to polystyrene. The thickness of the polystyrene introduces the additional factor of relief and in relation to the whiteness of the polystyrene this means that shadows become important. Straight cuts into a tile are best made with a knife whilst curved shapes can be cut out by the hot wire method.

Figures 66 and 67 are extended designs made from rectangular tiles. These exercises rely on cutting and spacing for their effect; all the parts are used, being glued to a paper backing.

Polystyrene is an ideal material from which to cut silhouettes and because of its soft character items can be impressed into its surface as well as glued to it. In figure 68 the fish silhouette has lines painted on it, shapes glued to it, and nails impressed into it.

Using manufactured shapes and offcuts

Particular shapes can be purchased from suppliers and these used to create a variety of interesting three-dimensional pictures, see figure 69.

Use can also be made of offcuts and discarded shapes and pieces, as in figure 70.

66 Extended design from a polystyrene tile

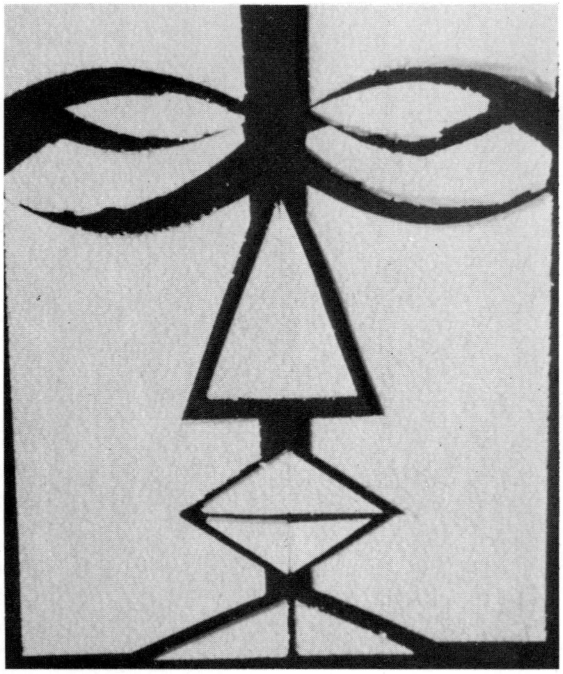

67 Extended design from a polystyrene tile

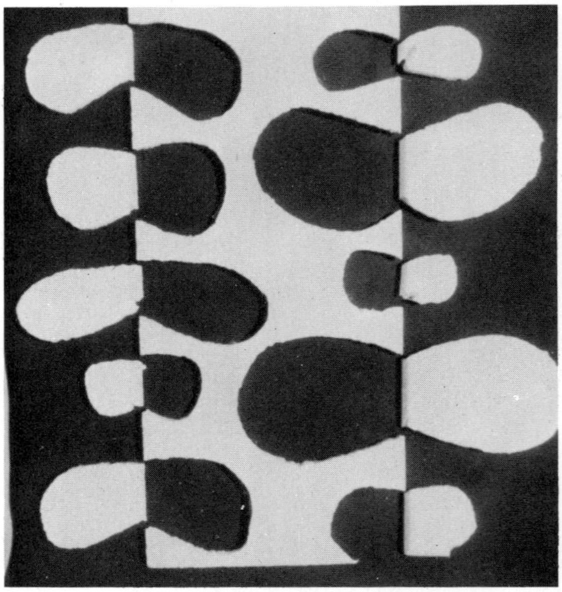

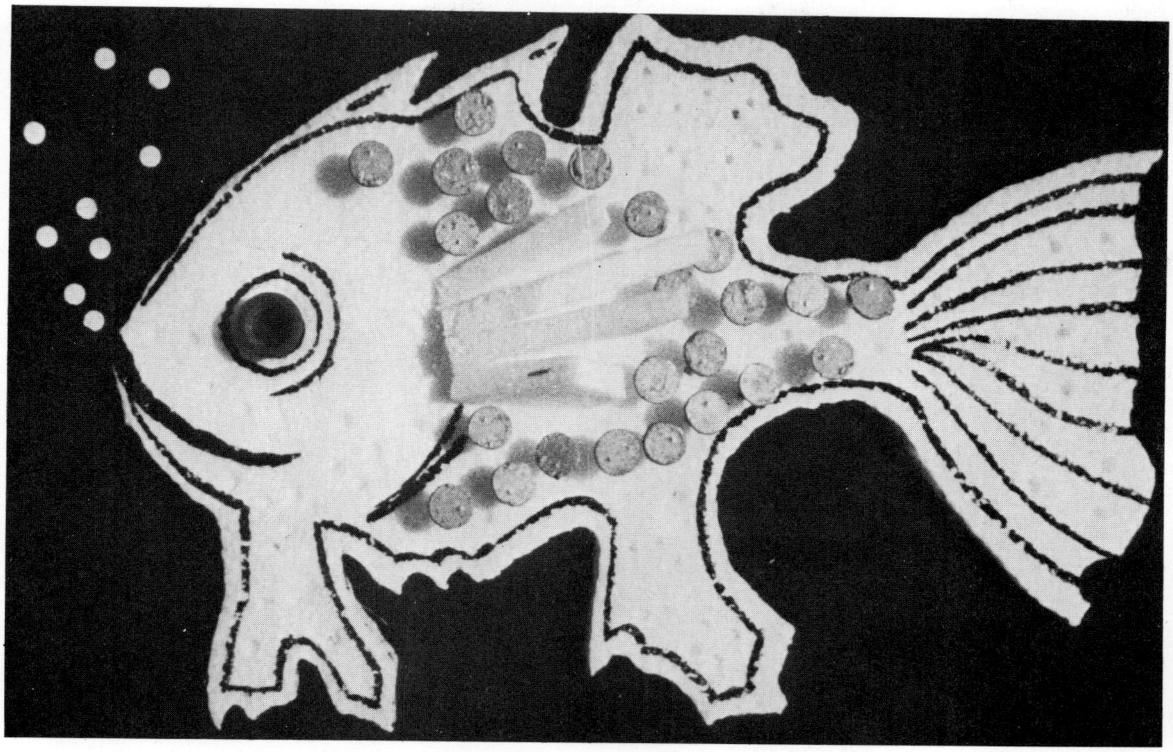

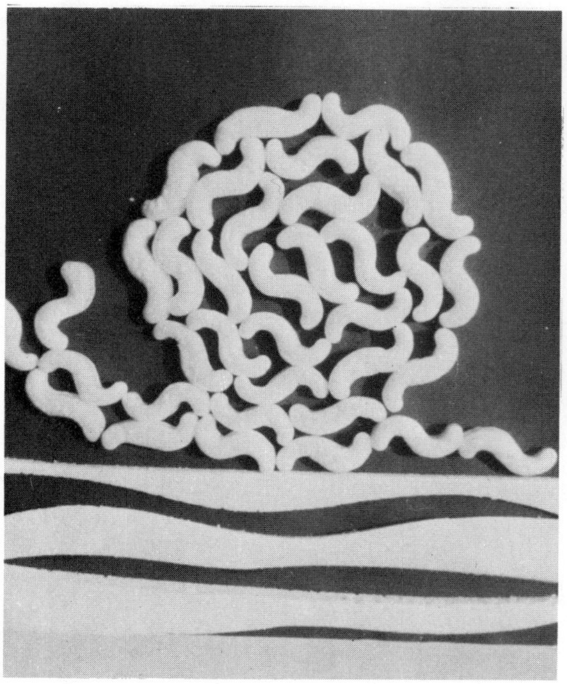

68 Polystyrene silhouette with added decoration

69 Designing with preshaped polystyrene pieces

Layers

As with cardboard and wood, relief can be achieved by building up in a series of layers. If some of the shapes are to be painted then use water-based paints. Colour could be introduced or use made of variations in light and dark.

Cellulose spray paints will eat into the surface of the polystyrene. Layers can be overlapped to produce very intense shadows. Some of the layers could have holes made in them or shapes impressed into their surface. Patterned polystyrene could also be used. Figure 71 consists of layered blocks and strips glued to a large tile. The hole in one of the layers on the left-hand side of the illustration was bored through the polystyrene by using a metal bolt, the end of which had been heated in a candle flame.

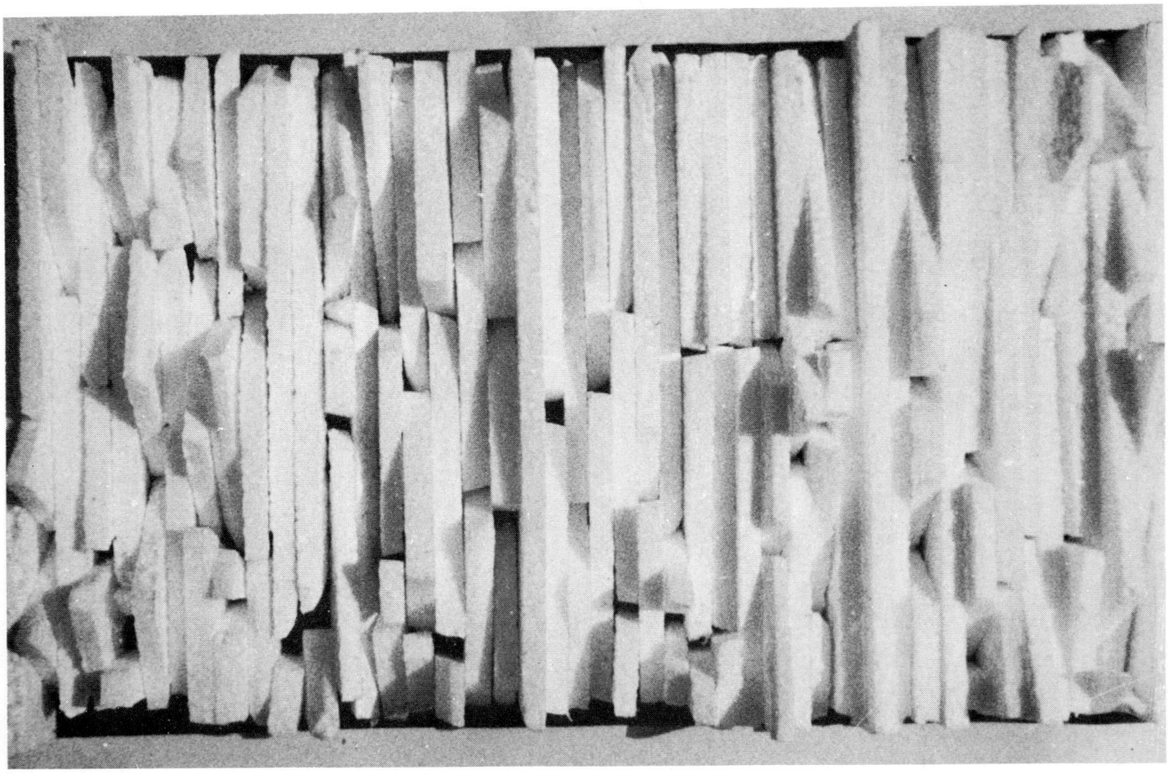

70 Using offcuts

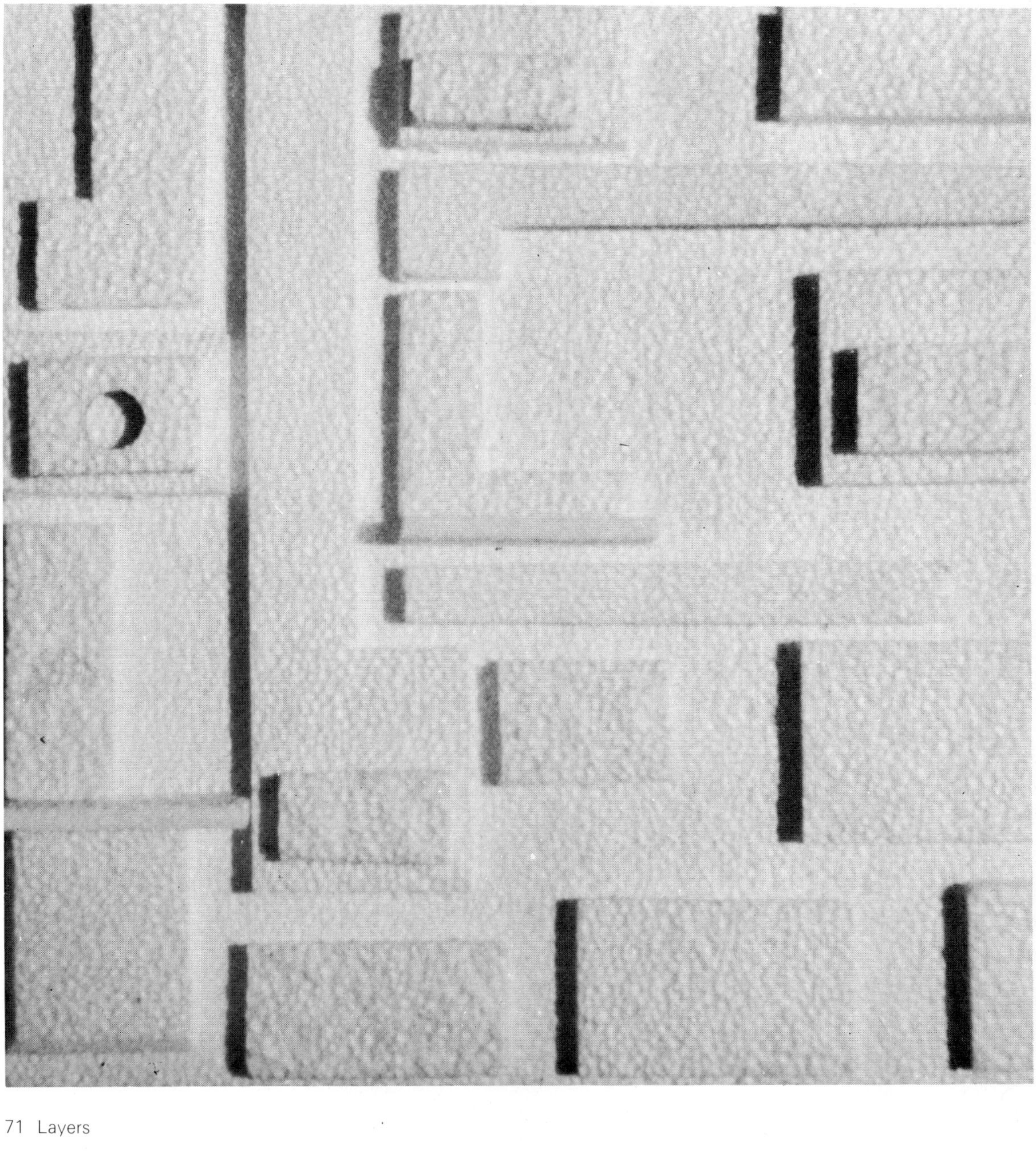

71 Layers

Assemblage pictures on a polystyrene tile base

Other items can be glued to a polystyrene tile to create a picture, as illustrated in figures 72 and 73. PVA adhesive will suit most materials. Allow ample time for the glue to dry before framing or displaying the work.

In figure 72 metal washers have been glued to the surface of a polystyrene tile which had previously had holes burnt through it using the method described for figure 71. Some of the holes were only partially burnt into the surface to give shallow indentations.

72 A drilled polystyrene tile with glued on shapes

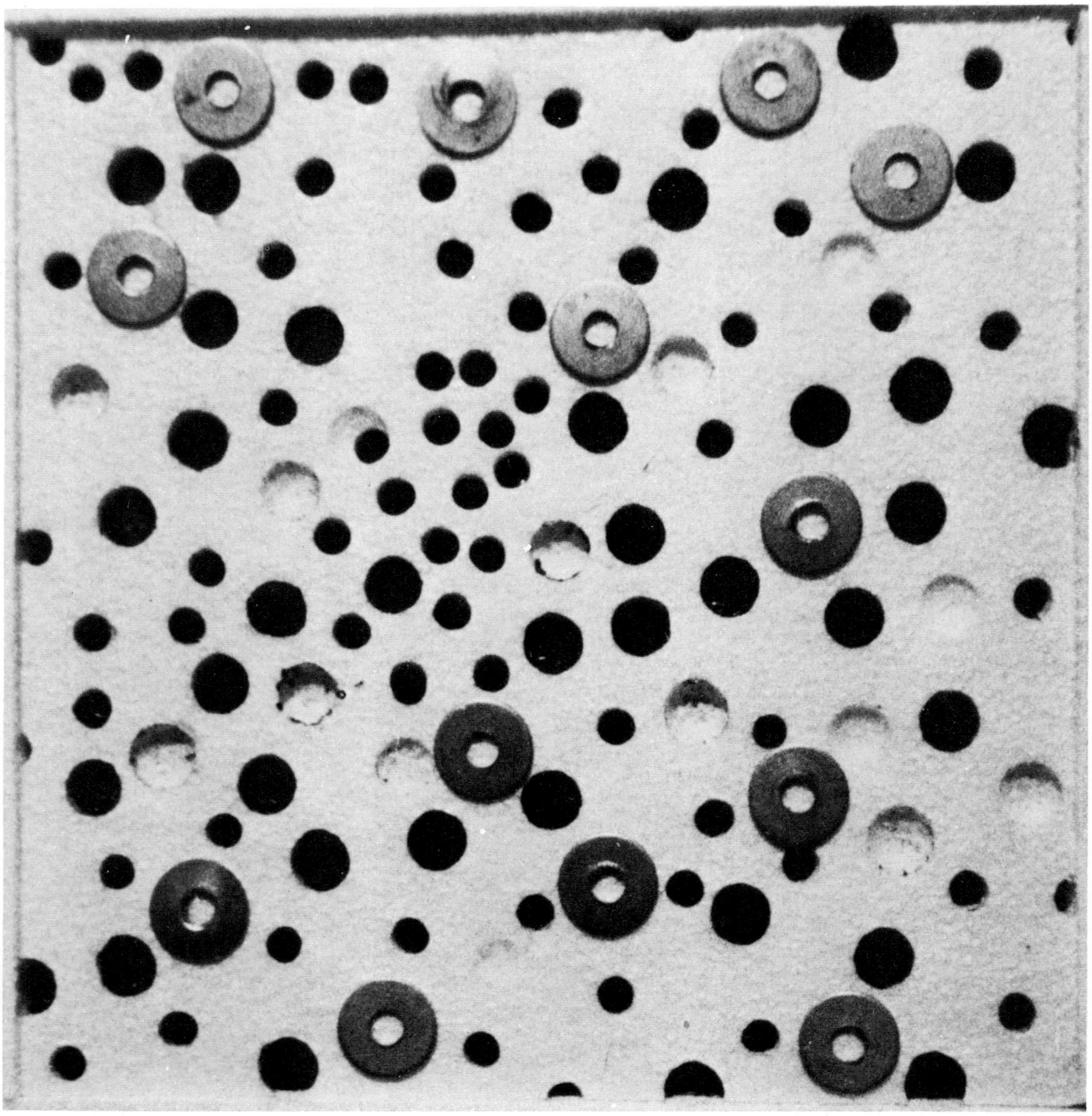

Figure 73 uses polystyrene shapes, bottle tops, felt nails and drawing pins (thumb tacks). The tops of the nails were painted with poster paint as were the lines on the body of the insect.

73 An assembled design on a polystyrene tile base

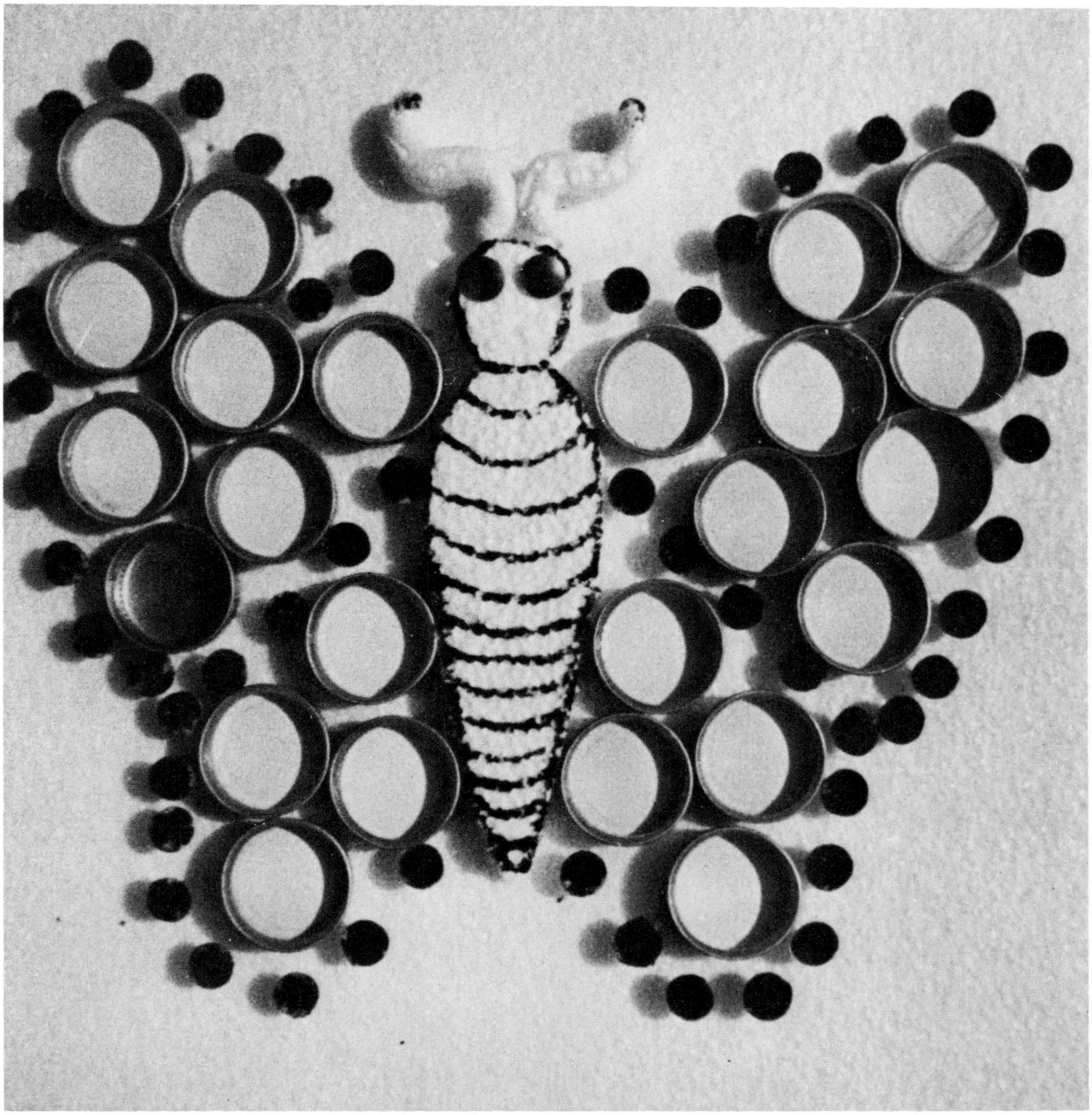

Pins and thread

Steel pins and most types of nails are easily pushed into the soft polystyrene surface. Pictures can be made by using various kinds of nails and pins and by making use of angles and directions, as described at the end of Section 4 of this book.

Figure 74 combines steel pins and cotton thread. Added interest is achieved by using different thicknesses and colours. See also figures 64 and 68.

Burning and cutting

The unused polystyrene tile can be transformed by the application of heat. Relief effects can be achieved by allowing the heat from a candle flame or bunsen burner to play on various parts of the surface causing burning, expansion and warping, as illustrated in figure 75. If the tile is held close to a candle flame it will pick up deposits of soot, a process which can be allied to the fumage techniques of collagists, see figure 76. All burning techniques should be performed in a well ventilated area.

74 Pins and thread

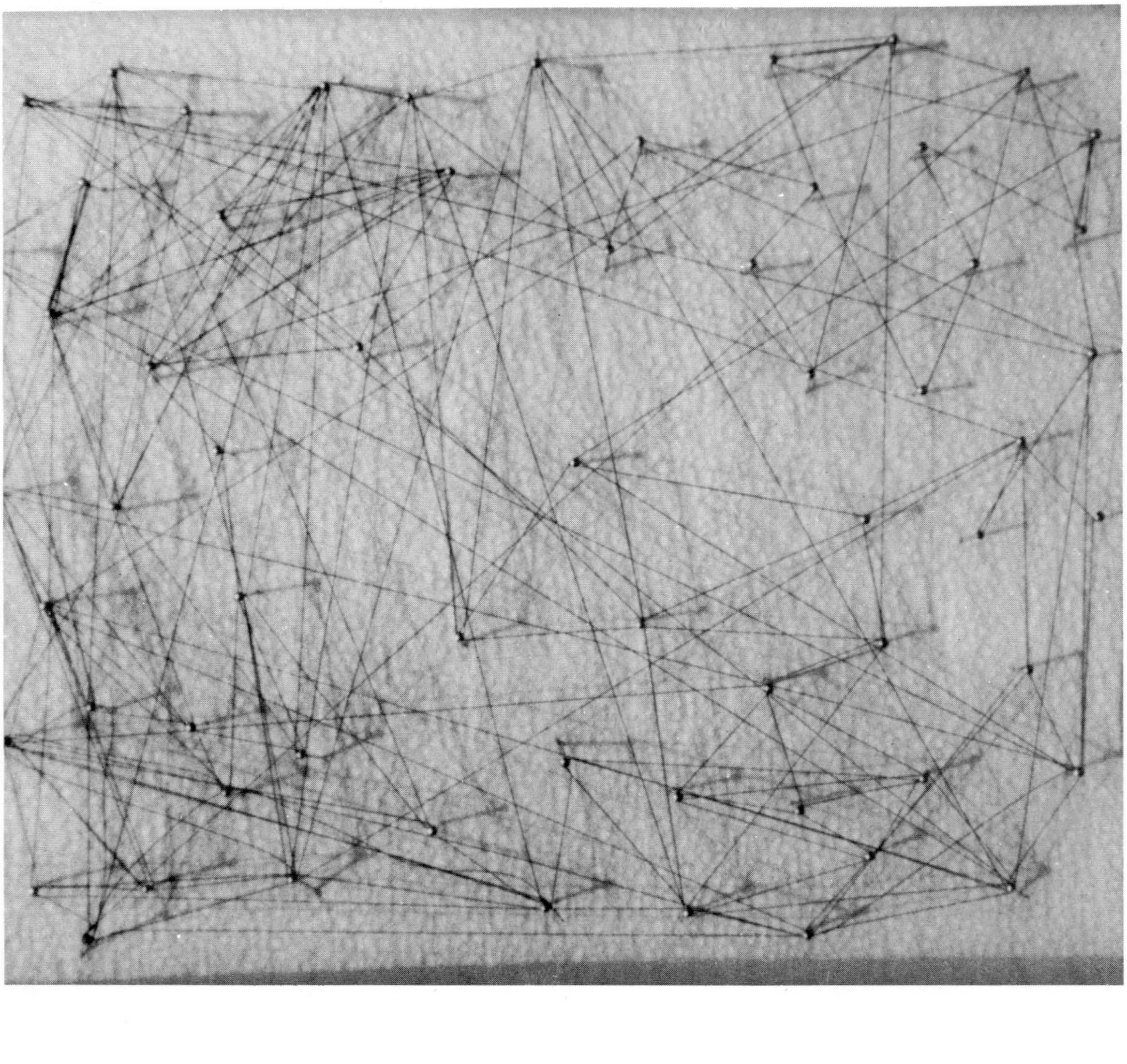

75 Applying heat

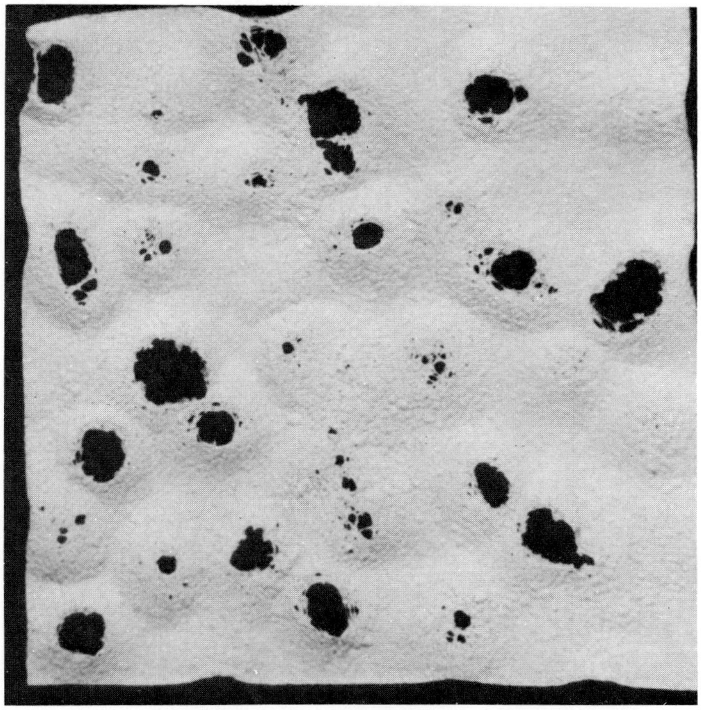

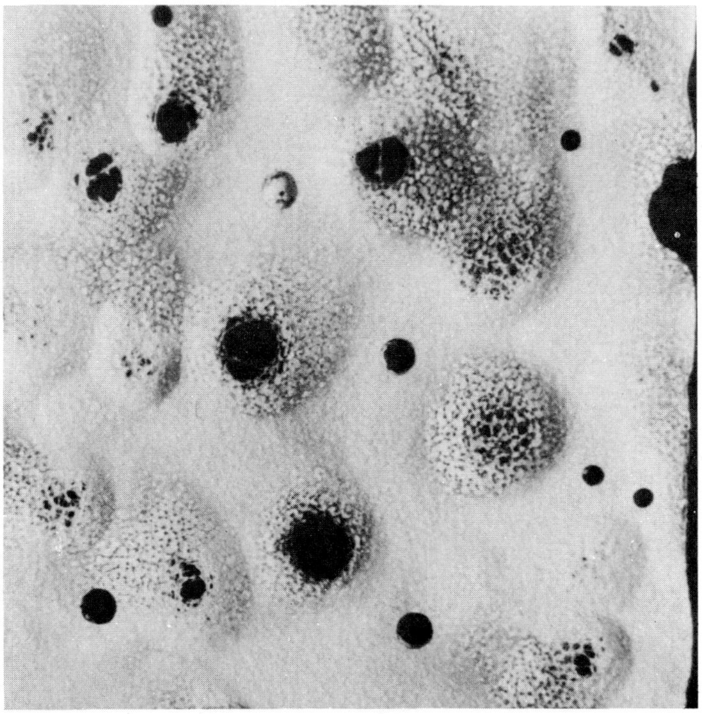

76 Heated and scorched design

Other materials

Paper, wood and expanded polystyrene are readily available to most people and this is why particular emphasis has been given to three-dimensional picture techniques using these materials. The ideas which have been described and illustrated in the previous three sections may, of course, be adapted to suit various other materials, whether gleaned from nature or the scrapyard, or purchased from a supplier or manufacturer. A craft book such as this has certain imposed limitations: it is hoped that the reader, having seen what can be done with inexpensive and easily obtained materials will exploit the pictorial possibilities of others. The reader is also urged to consult books which cover particular crafts or technical processes or which investigate the use of certain materials. Recommendations for further reading and research are made at the back of this book.

The fundamental issues which have been covered, whether concerned with the aesthetic qualities of the picture or the methods involved in making it, will equally well apply to any materials. Most of the ideas described so far have been based on the principle of sticking shapes to a backing support. Many other materials can be involved to create low-relief or more pronounced three-dimensional pictures by employing this technique and some of these are described in this section.

In designing a picture the selection of a specific material may be governed by various factors. Its colour, texture and thickness must be considered as well as its technical suitability, that is whether it can be glued or fixed in some way. Use can be made of contrasts in surface textures, different shapes and variations in relief. In pictorial work a certain material might be chosen because it suits the characteristics of a particular animal, for example, or the texture of an object. See figures 63 and 78.

Methods of working, planning the design, the choice of the support and adhesive are all important and must relate to individual materials. Choose a support which is strong enough to take the weight of whatever materials are to be glued to it and which will not be distorted by the gluing or fixing technique. Plywood or hardboard *(Masonite)* is recommended as backing for most pictures. Where large pictures are envisaged the hardboard may need strengthening by backing it with lengths of wood; this is described on page 39.

String

Small string designs can be made on a thick cardboard support; larger, low-relief pictures can be built up on stretched canvas or prepared hardboard or plywood. The support can be sized or primed prior to use and may need painting a particular colour or involve a basic painted design which is subsequently further developed by the addition of string. Such pictures can use different types of string as well as raffia, thread, wool, rope, wire and so on. Contrasts of colour and thickness can be used and these combined with various techniques such as coiling, fraying and knotting. Sisal, cotton, nylon and polypropylene are some of the different kinds of string, whilst fibreglass, wool and animal hair have similar characteristics. In designing a picture with string it is often best to apply the glue to the support and then impress the string into this, perhaps holding it in place with some form of weight until the glue has dried. Use a non-staining, clear adhesive such as PVA or *Marvin Medium*. Respect the nature of the material; string often displays a positive will to bend in a certain direction. Exploit this characteristic.

In figure 77 the string is used on a canvas support to form a large, powerful linear design; this example measures 178 cm × 244 cm (70 in. × 102 in.). This work exploits contrasts of spacing and is perhaps inspired from natural forms such as wood grain. Children enjoy making simple linear designs in this way. The use of white string on black paper can be most effective.

Coiled string and thread has been used in figure 78, a technique in character with this particular animal. Different colours and types of string have been used in figure 79 in a design which allows the free-flowing nature of this material to be realised. Figure 80 is an appliqué design using string, thread and wool combined with fabric, whilst in figure 81 string has been used with various allied materials.

77 Gwyther Irwin: *Stringent.* String on canvas

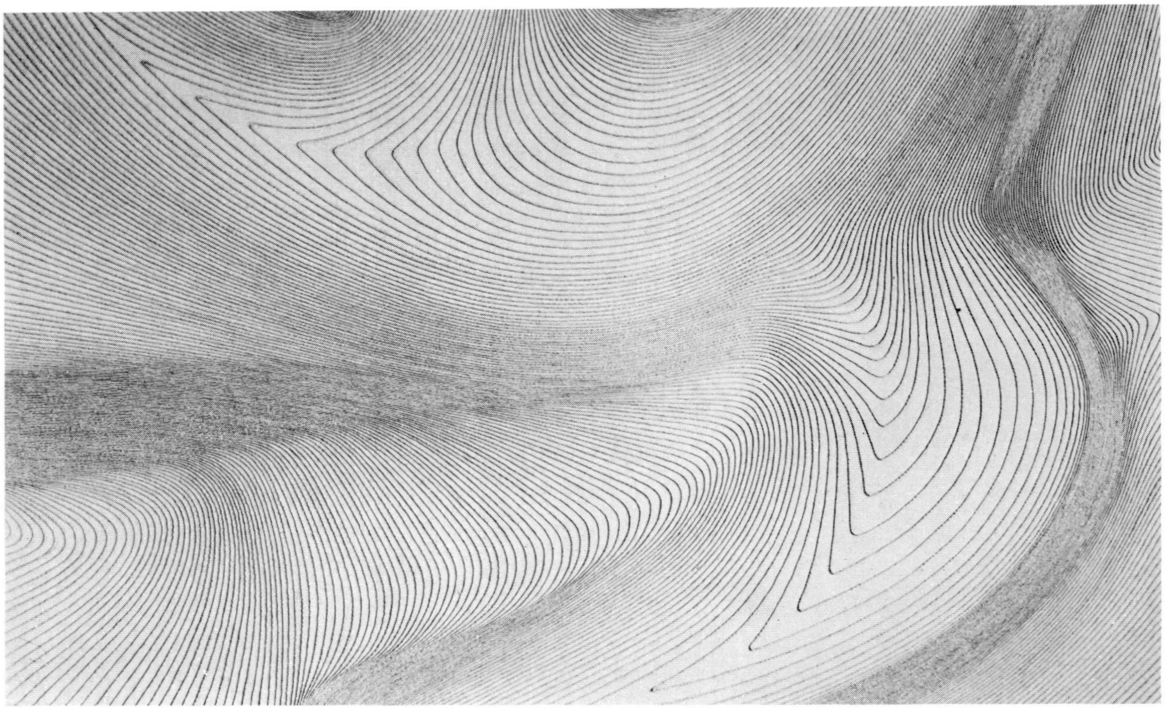

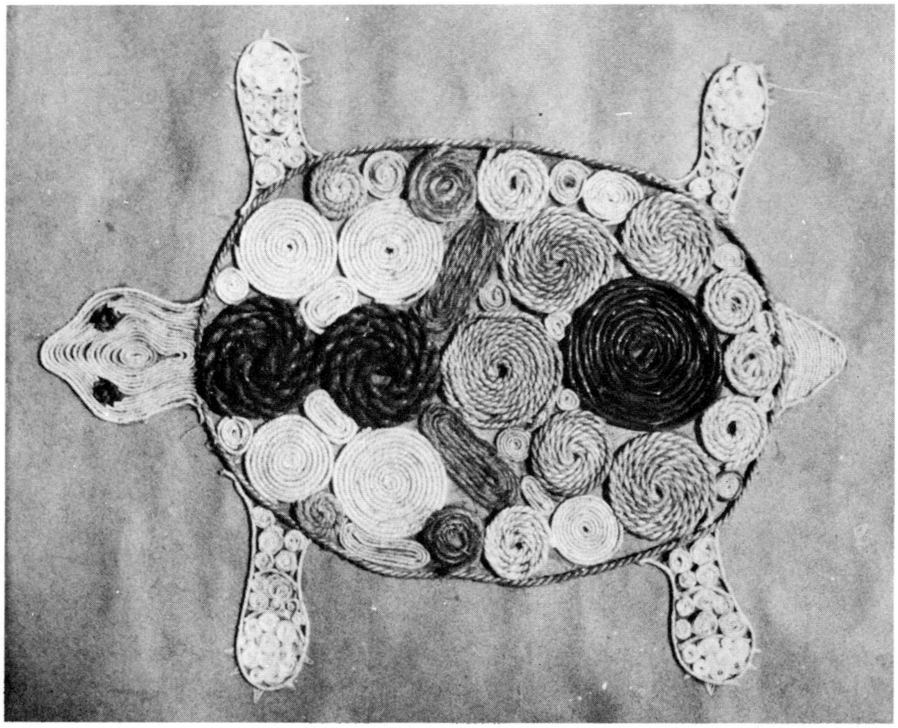

78 String design

79 String design

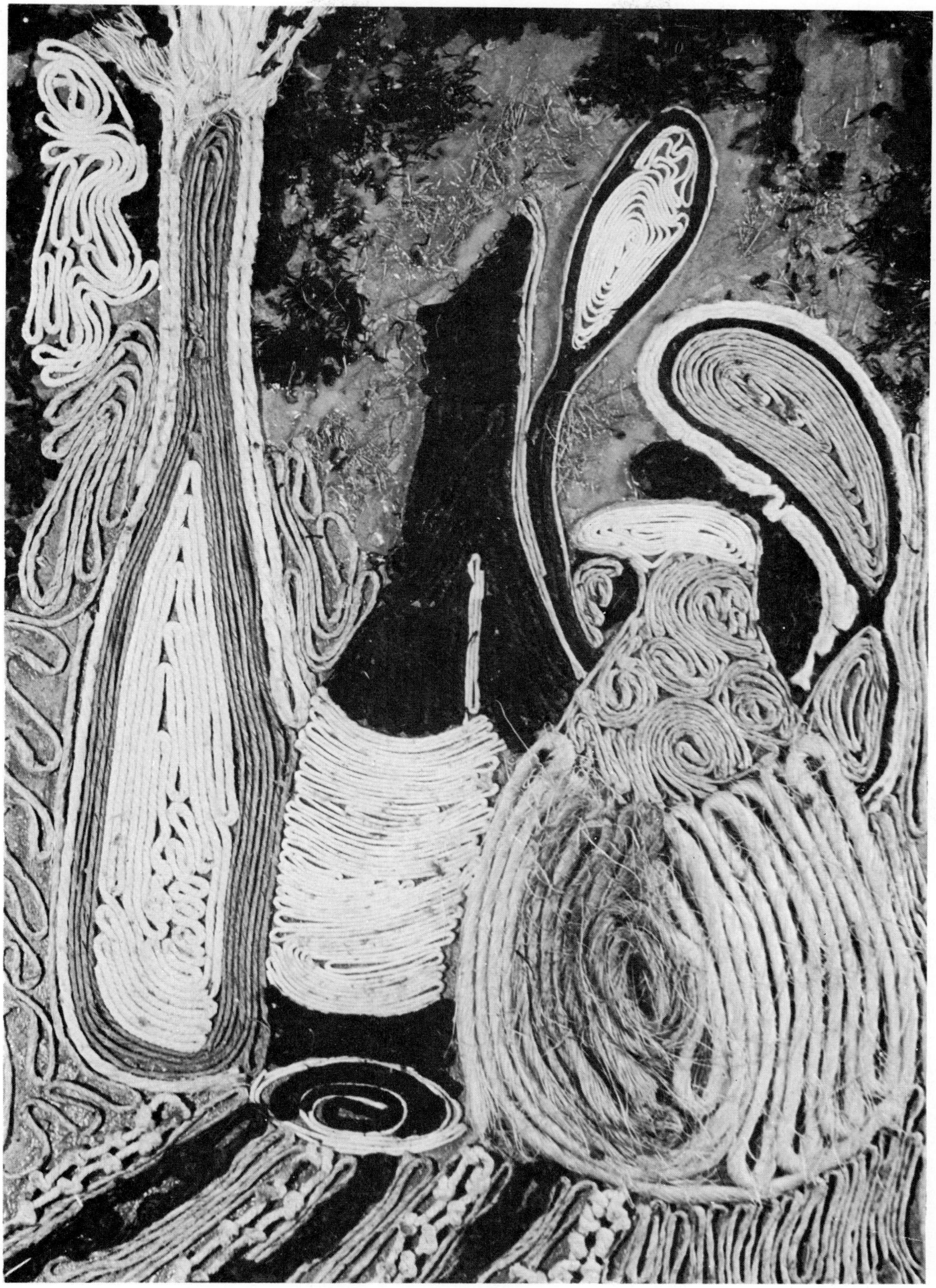

80 Fabric, string and wool

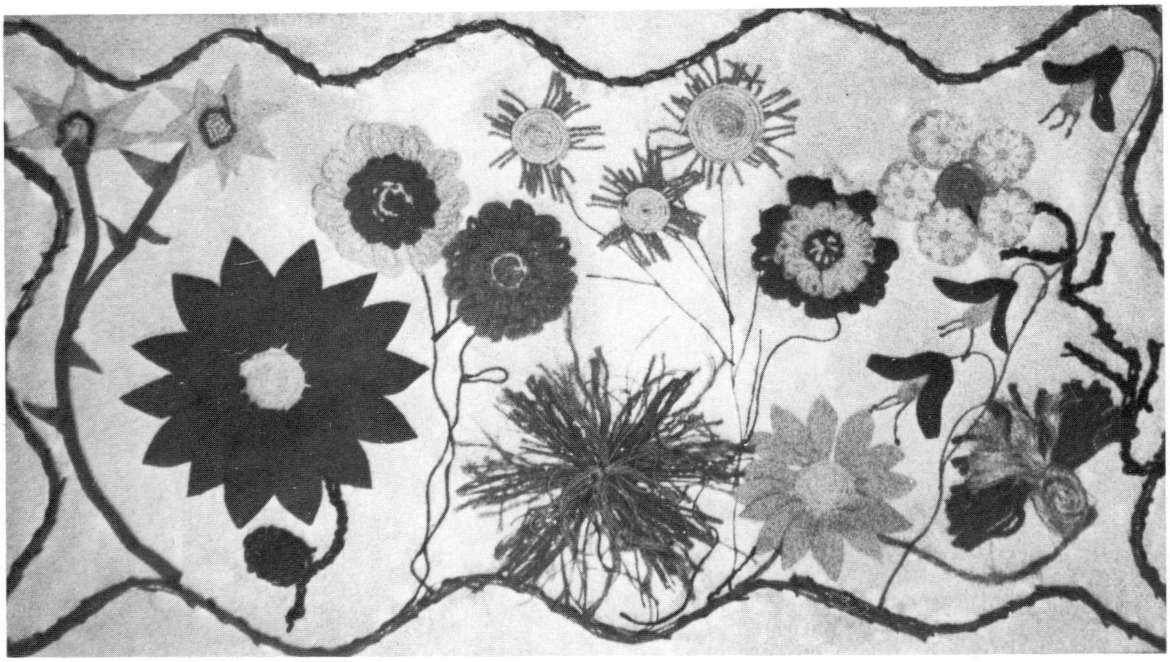

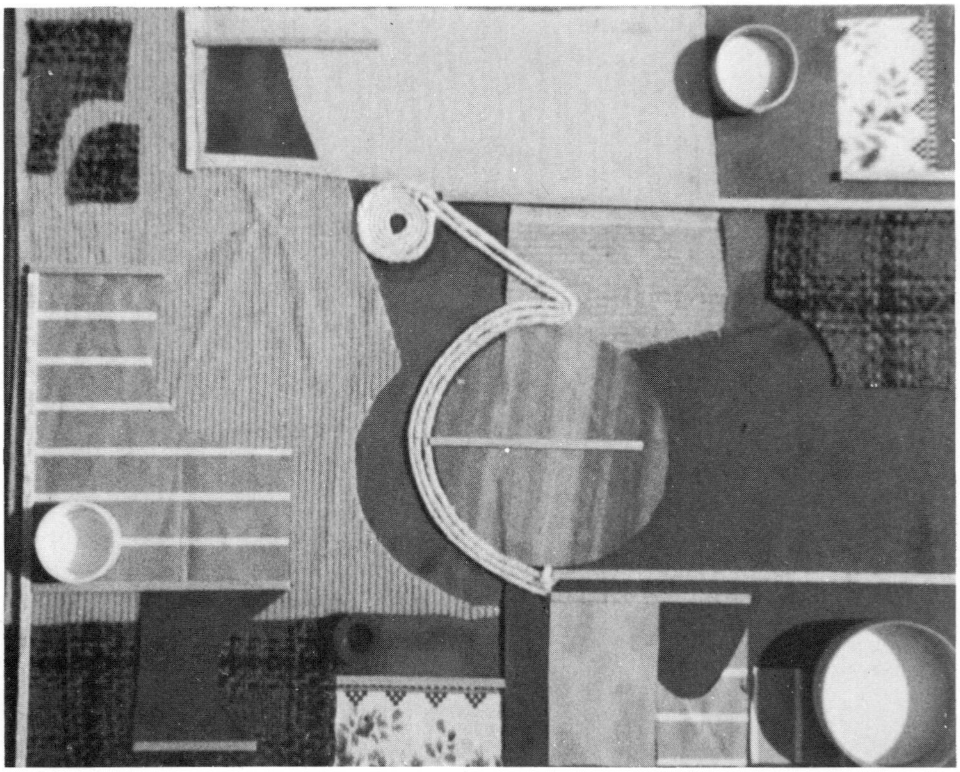

81 Fabric, string and other materials

Fabric

Fabric can be glued to a support in collage form or stitched to a suitable backing to make an appliqué design. If a canvas or stretched hessian support is used, then the two methods can be combined. *Copydex* and PVA adhesives are once again the most suitable as they allow freedom of technique and dry quickly and transparently. The three-dimensional aspect of the work can be enhanced by incorporating other materials, for example string, beads and buttons, or by employing a technique like ruffling or smocking which will allow greater protrusion of the material from its flat backing surface. Fabric remnants such as upholstery scraps, printed fabrics, leather, towelling and hessian are ideal for use. See figures 82 to 84.

Pin and thread craft is allied to these techniques and has become very popular. The support will normally have to be of soft wood, such as plywood, so as to give adequate hold to the steel pins which will otherwise be pulled out of place by the taut thread. If desired, the board can be covered with fabric, painted, or decorated in some other way prior to use. Mathematical designs, like the one illustrated in figure 85, are very suitable but this is not to say that these exclude freer methods of treatment. Such logical designs obviously need carefully planning and the position of the steel pins must be marked before they are gently tapped into the board. The pins only need knocking in to a depth which holds them firm; the remainder of their length will therefore protrude from the surface and allow various layers of thread to be used, thus exploiting the three-dimensional possibilities.

Steel pins are available in various types and lengths and these can be combined with thread of different thicknesses and colours.

See also figure 74.

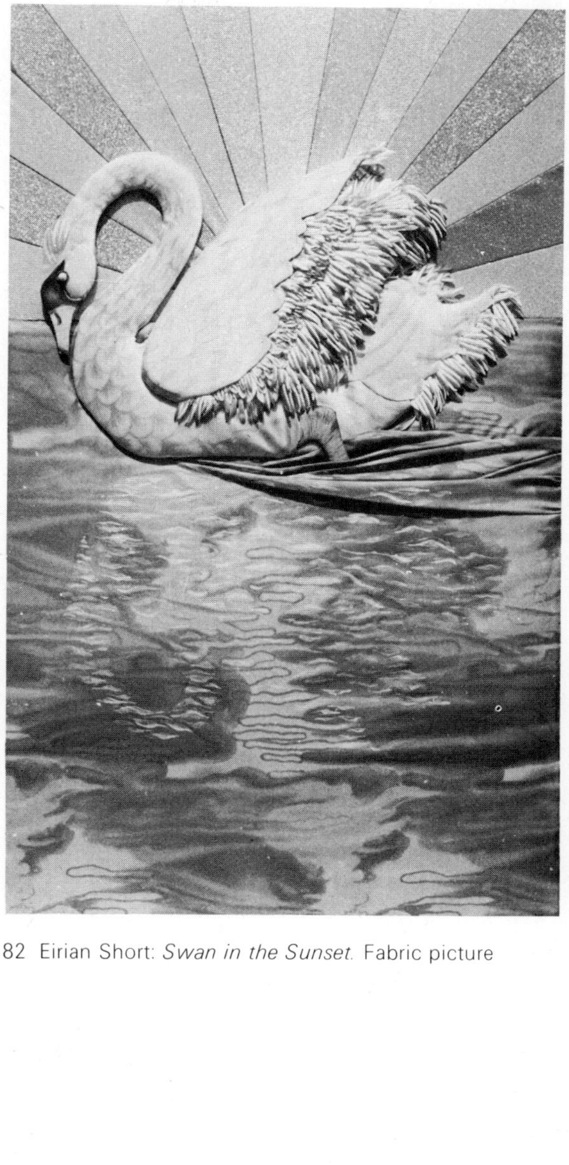

82 Eirian Short: *Swan in the Sunset*. Fabric picture

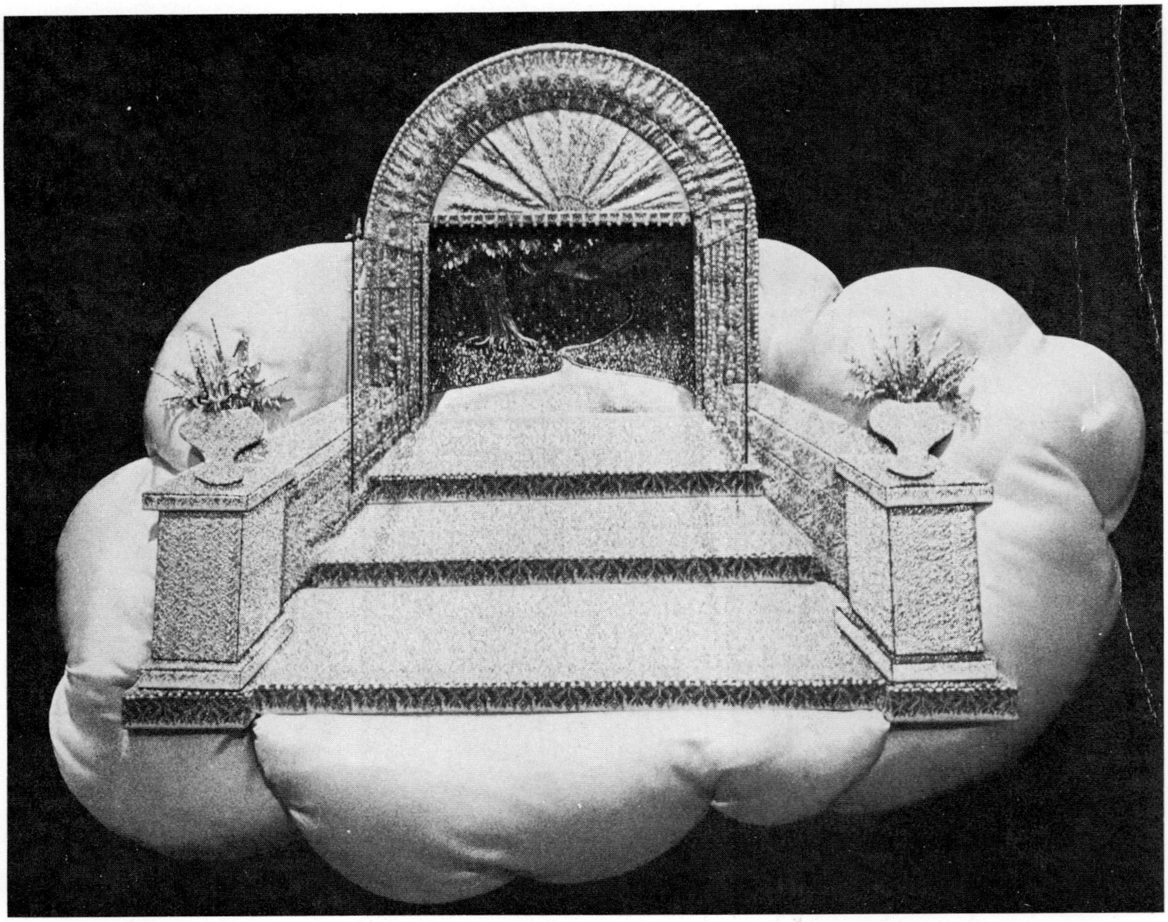

83 Eirian Short: *Pearly Gates.* Fabric picture

84 Margaret Thom: *Flower Garden.* Smocking

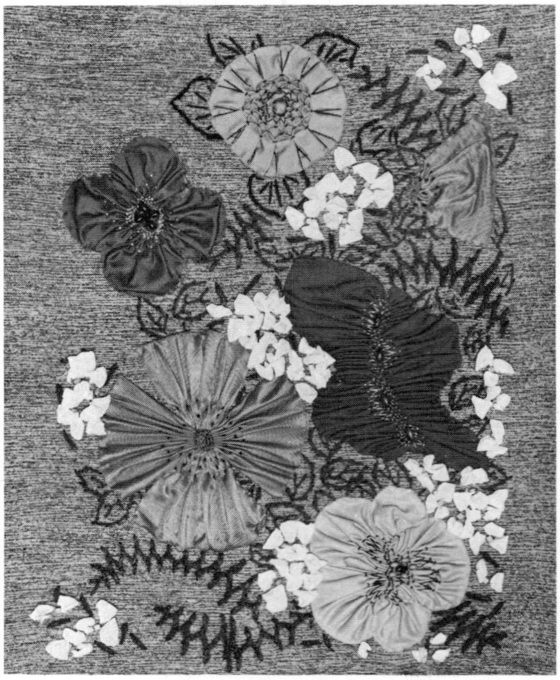

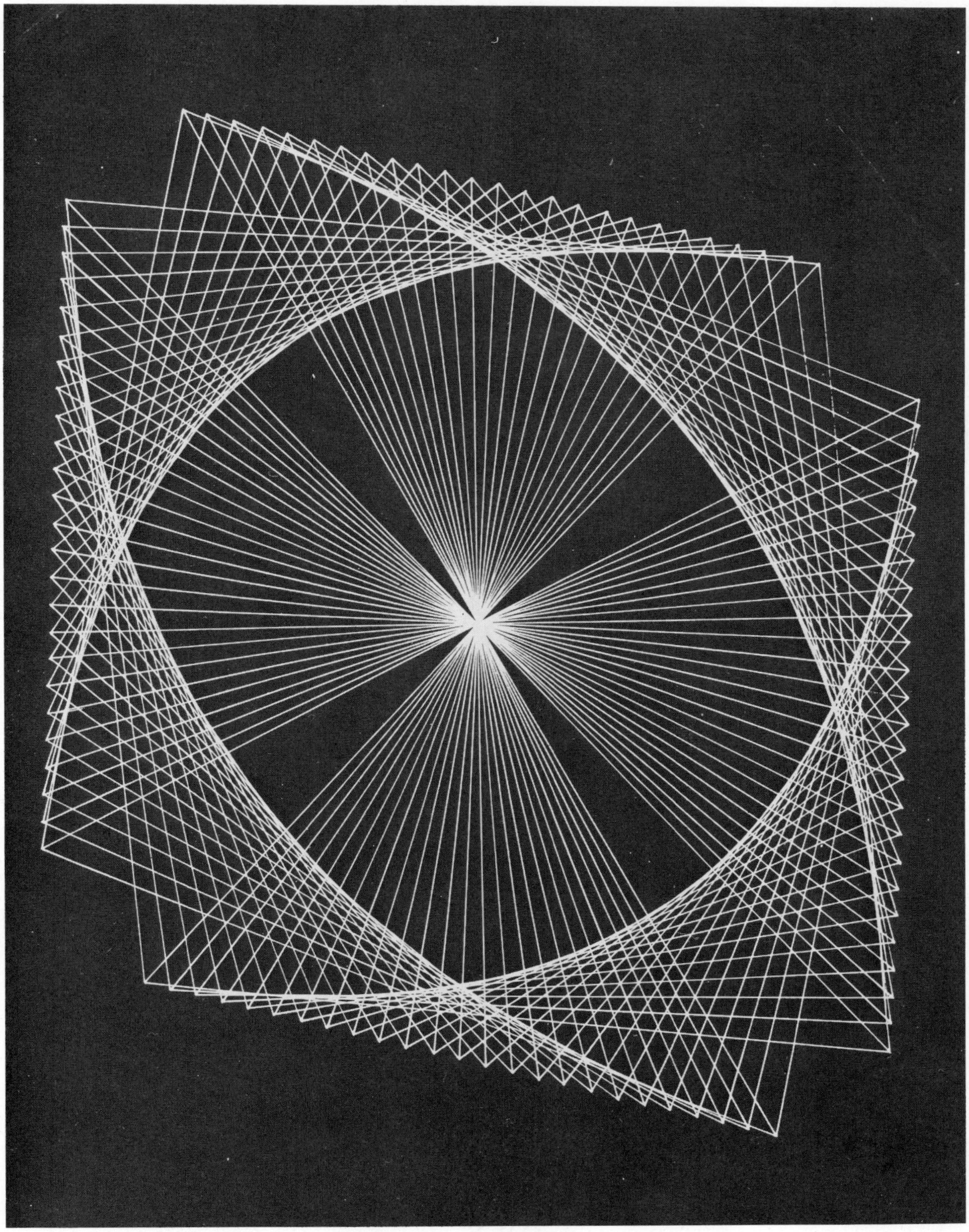

85 Warren Farnworth: pin and thread design

Scrap and found material

Many items of household waste, for example lids, cartons, cardboard boxes, corrugated paper and plastic bottles and containers have a possible use for three-dimensional picture making. These items could be used in their 'found' state or perhaps cut up to form new shapes and brush or spray painted. Natural materials such as twigs, bark, straw and leaves could also be used. Indeed, with modern adhesives, screwing, nailing, or perhaps some other device such as welding or soldering, and the construction of special supports it is possible to fix almost any material to a backing, as in figures 98 to 100.

In figure 86 bottle tops have been glued to a hardboard support to form an abstract design. Notice how the shadows play an effective part in this work. Shapes, sizes and colours may also be used with significance.

Metal has not previously been mentioned because it is a material which is normally expensive and fairly difficult to obtain and because its use demands certain skills and specialised equipment. However, some scrap metals, for example used tin cans and tin lids, can be put to creative use. Welded tins (empty fruit or soup cans), galvanized tin, copper and brass can be cold-soldered. Items can be soldered together as well as to a metal support. The alternative to soldering is to use a suitable adhesive such as *Araldite*.

For soldering, an electric soldering-iron will be required as well as solder, flux and sal-ammoniac. Inspect the pieces of metal to be joined and ensure that they are free of grease and dirt. If necessary, clean the metals with a file or emery-cloth. Flux is applied to the surface before soldering them together. Allow the solder to set before moving the work. Most soldering-irons have a copper bit which will periodically need cleaning with sal-ammoniac or a file.

Other metals, large tin lids for example, or thin sheets of copper, brass, zinc or tin, can be used for embossing and repoussé techniques. Strips of these materials can be used for many of the ideas described for using strips of wood. Cut the tin with a pair of goldsmith's scissors. By placing the sheet tin on a soft, padded surface, it can easily be worked with a hammer or with special chasing and embossing tools. Use a metal-punch or a large nail to make holes in thin metal surfaces.

Natural materials have become a popular source of inspiration for collage and assemblage work and examples are illustrated in figures 89 to 97. Select good specimens for this work and ensure that they are dry and as clean as possible. As before, most of these materials are easily attached with PVA glue to a suitable backing material. Dried leaves, straw, twigs, bark, feathers and shells can be used in their 'found' state. Freshly picked leaves will need pressing between layers of absorbent paper for at least twenty-four hours before they are suitable for use. Completed work can be sprayed with a clear varnish as an added protection.

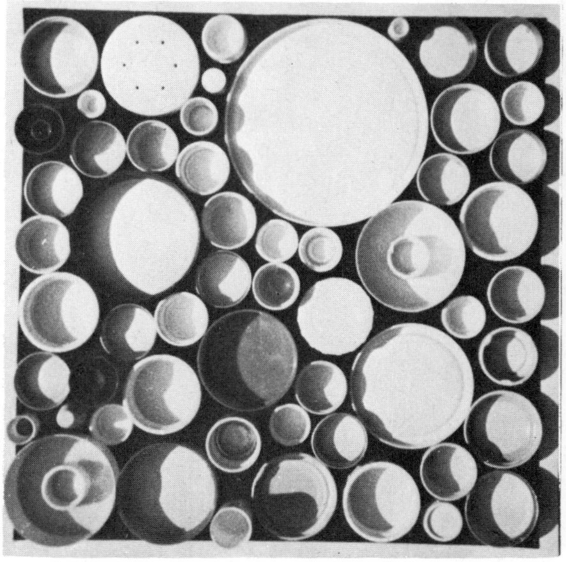

86 Bottle tops

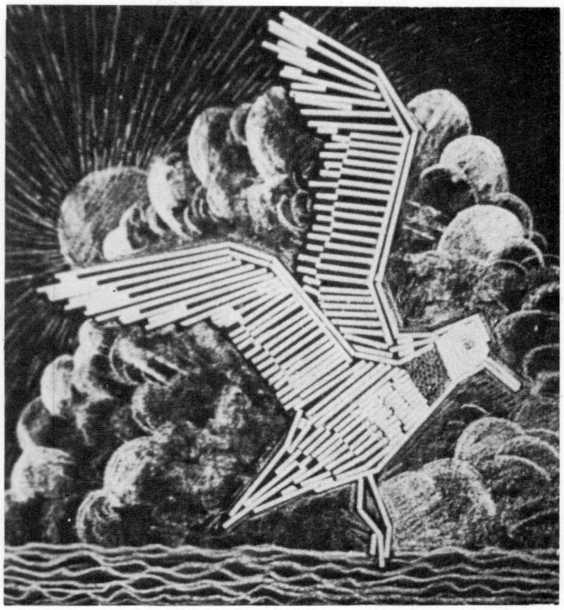

88 Drinking straws

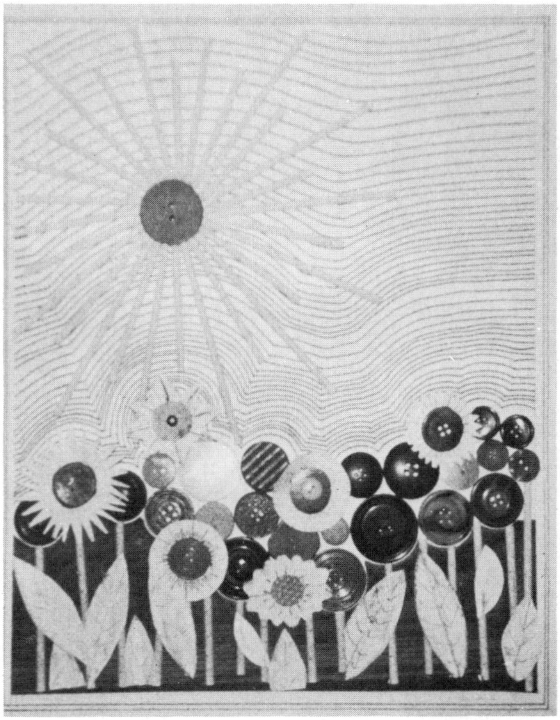

87 Buttons, drinking straws and other materials

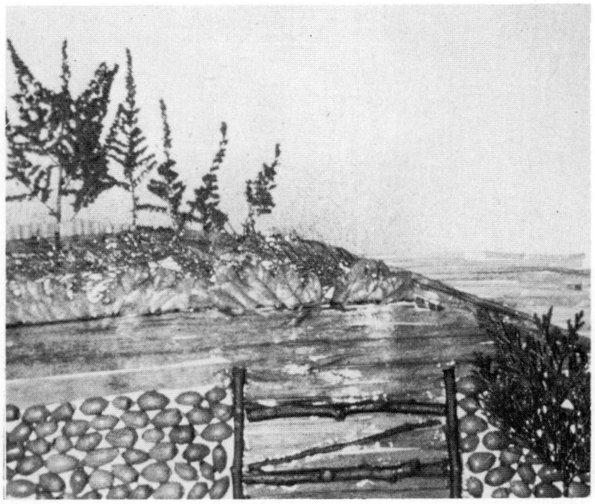

89 Dried leaves and natural materials

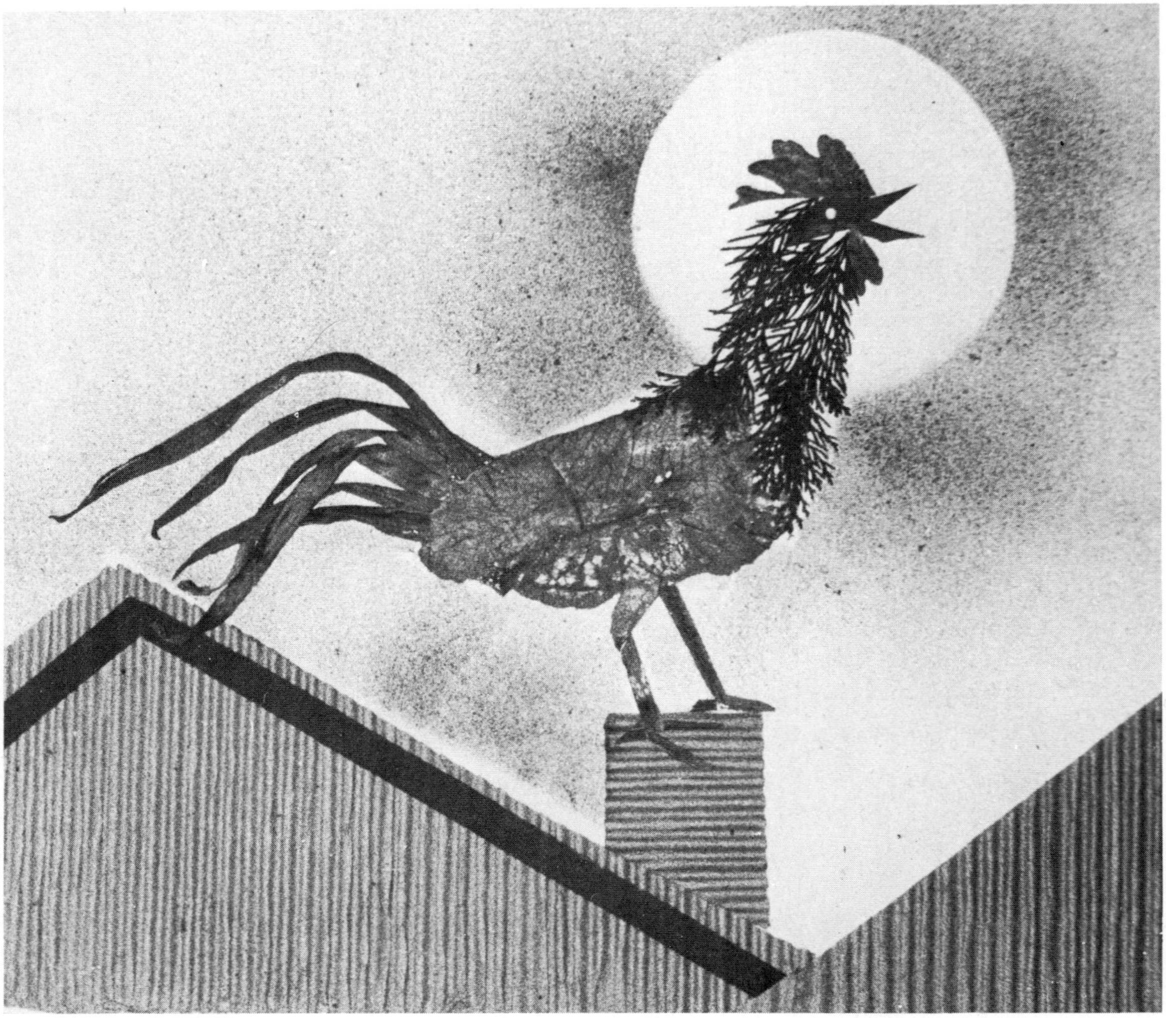

90 Leaves and corrugated paper

91 Detail from figure 90

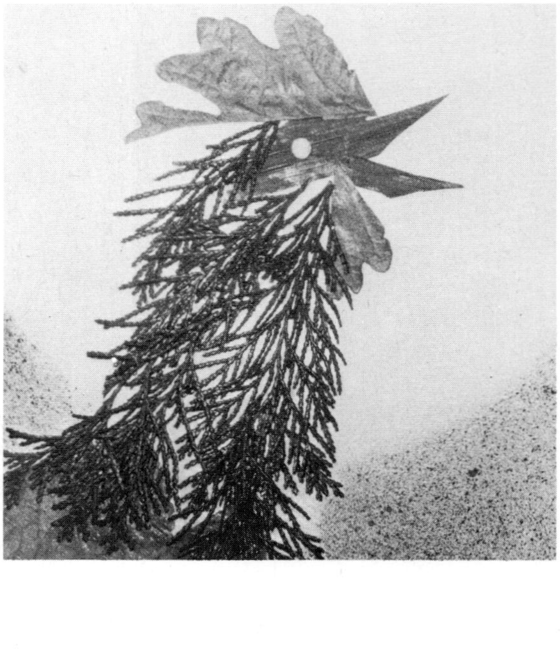

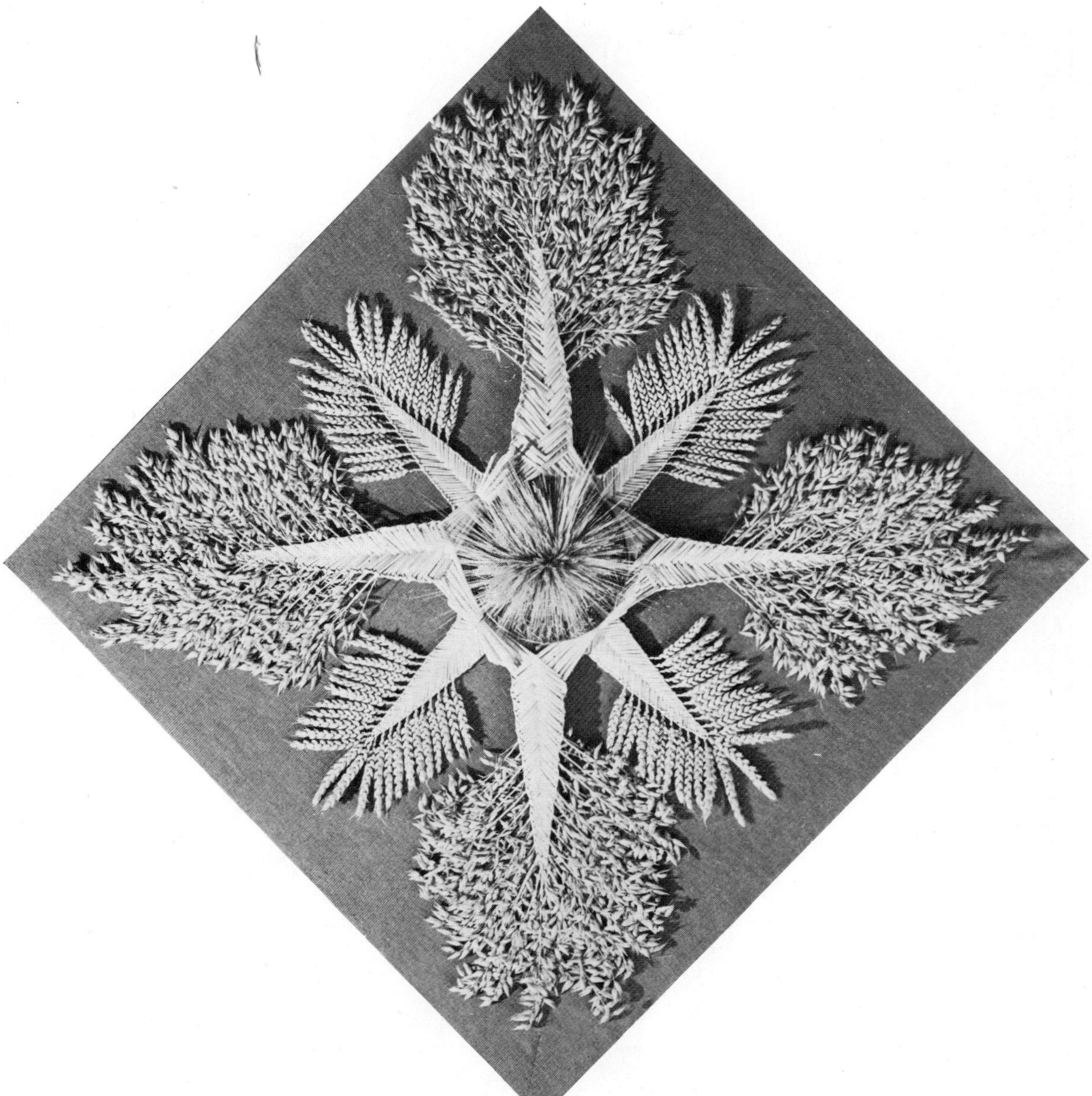

92 *Workman's Star.* Corn dolly

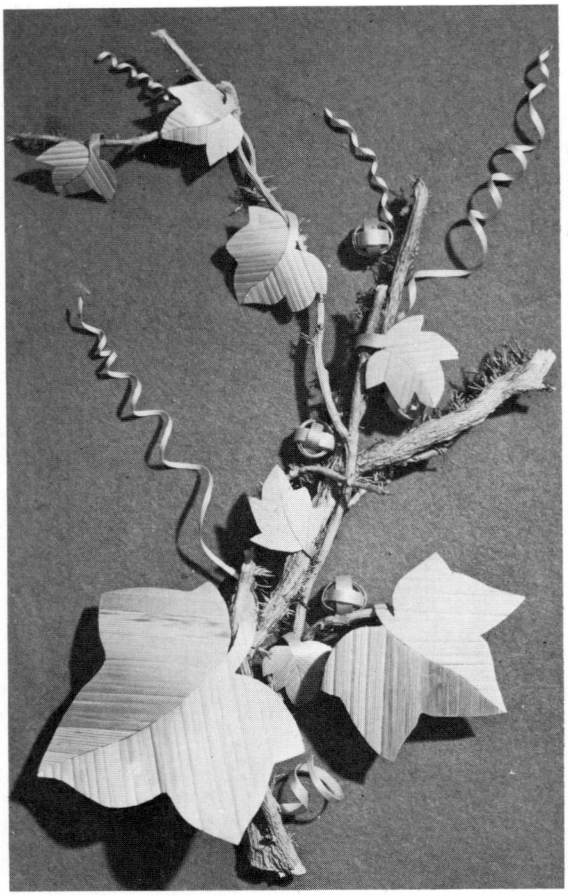

93 Ivy leaves, Marquetry collage

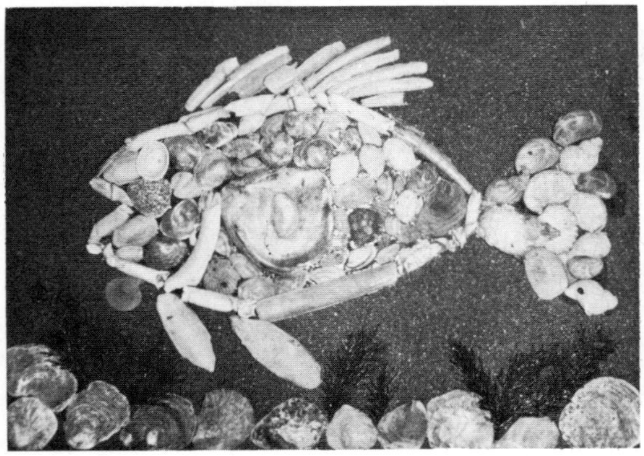

94 Shell collage

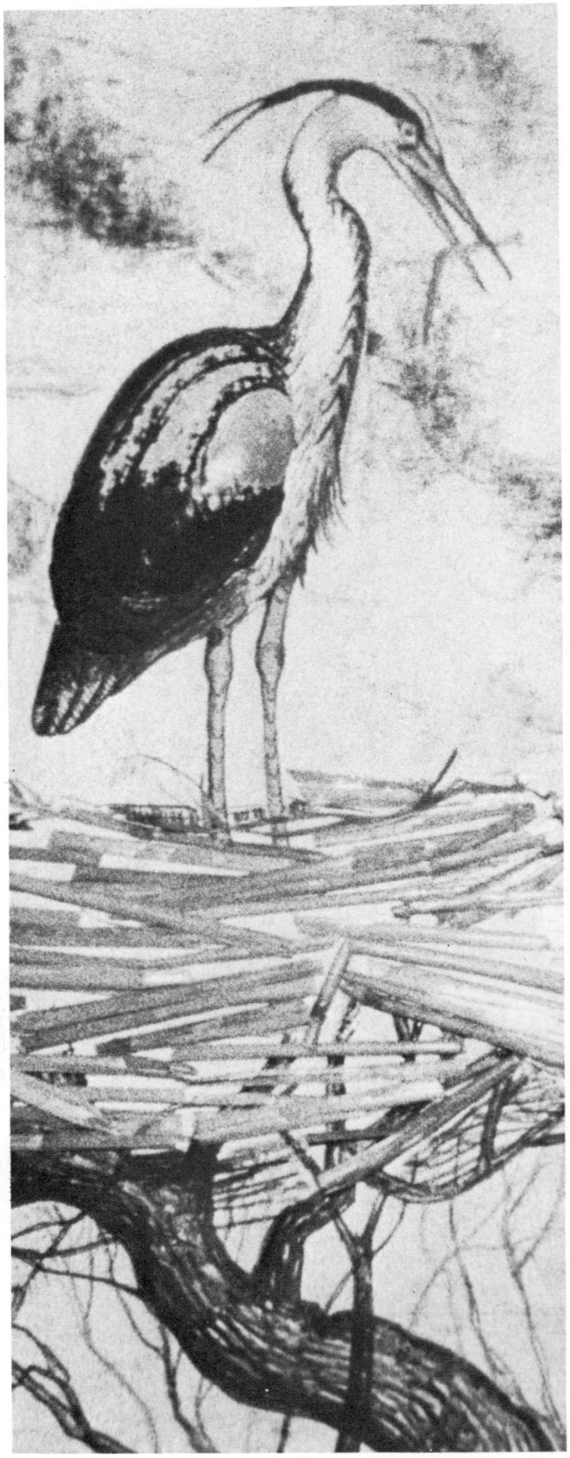

95 Natural materials

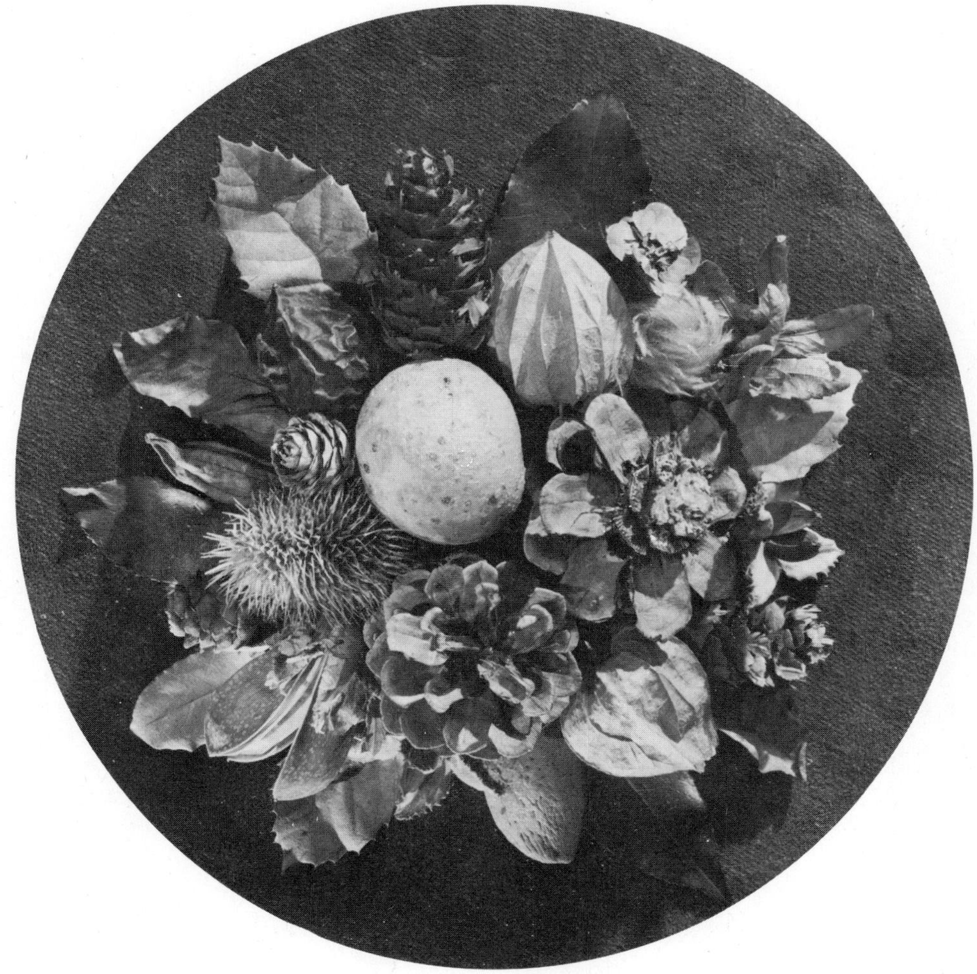

96 Julia Clements: plaque of dried flowers and leaves

Other techniques

The most obvious method of attaching shapes to a backing to make a three-dimensional picture is to use a suitable adhesive. Most of the ideas described so far in this book rely on this technique. Given the appropriate material as a backing support, shapes could also be stapled on with a stapler or tacker, pinned on with drawing pins or steel pins, sewn on, nailed or screwed, or inserted through slots. Most of these techniques have been mentioned and illustrated in the previous text. All of these methods place emphasis on an assemblage technique which in a sense is similar to painting except that the shapes one is using to design the picture are three-dimensional. Relatively little thought may be given to the support, save that it must suit whatever is to be glued to it. The final section of this book is therefore devoted to ways of constructing special supports or methods of texturing or altering the surface appearance of existing supports.

Cutting into the support

Various materials, if used as a support, can be cut into with a sharp knife, gouge, chisel, carving tool or saw. Indentations made in this way will obviously create a variable relief surface and this can be combined in the normal way with assemblage techniques or developed as a three-dimensional picture device in its own right. Points which have already been made about painting, shadows and so on will apply just as equally to an incised relief design as to one which has been built up from a flat surface.

Plywood, composition board, hardboard and most other boards can be cut into with the tools mentioned as well as have holes drilled into or through them with a hand or electric drill. Perforated and textured boards are also available and these could be used as an alternative to the flat surface varieties.

Clay and plaster are two other materials which readily invite cuts and impressions to be made into their soft surfaces. Engraved designs are possible from tiles of clay or plaster which, when dry and after glazing or painting, can be mounted on a plywood backing and displayed. Plaster tiles can be made by pouring the mixed plaster into a cardboard lid, such as a shoe-box lid. When the plaster has almost dried out it is possible to carve into it or impress objects into its surface. Do not attempt designs which are larger than 380 mm (15 in.) square or more than 25 mm (1 in.) thick, as the plaster is likely to crack. In any case, allow the plaster to dry in an even temperature and away from draughts. Clay tiles are made from prepared clay which is rolled

97 Shellwork octagonal panel. Early nineteenth century
Victoria and Albert Museum, London

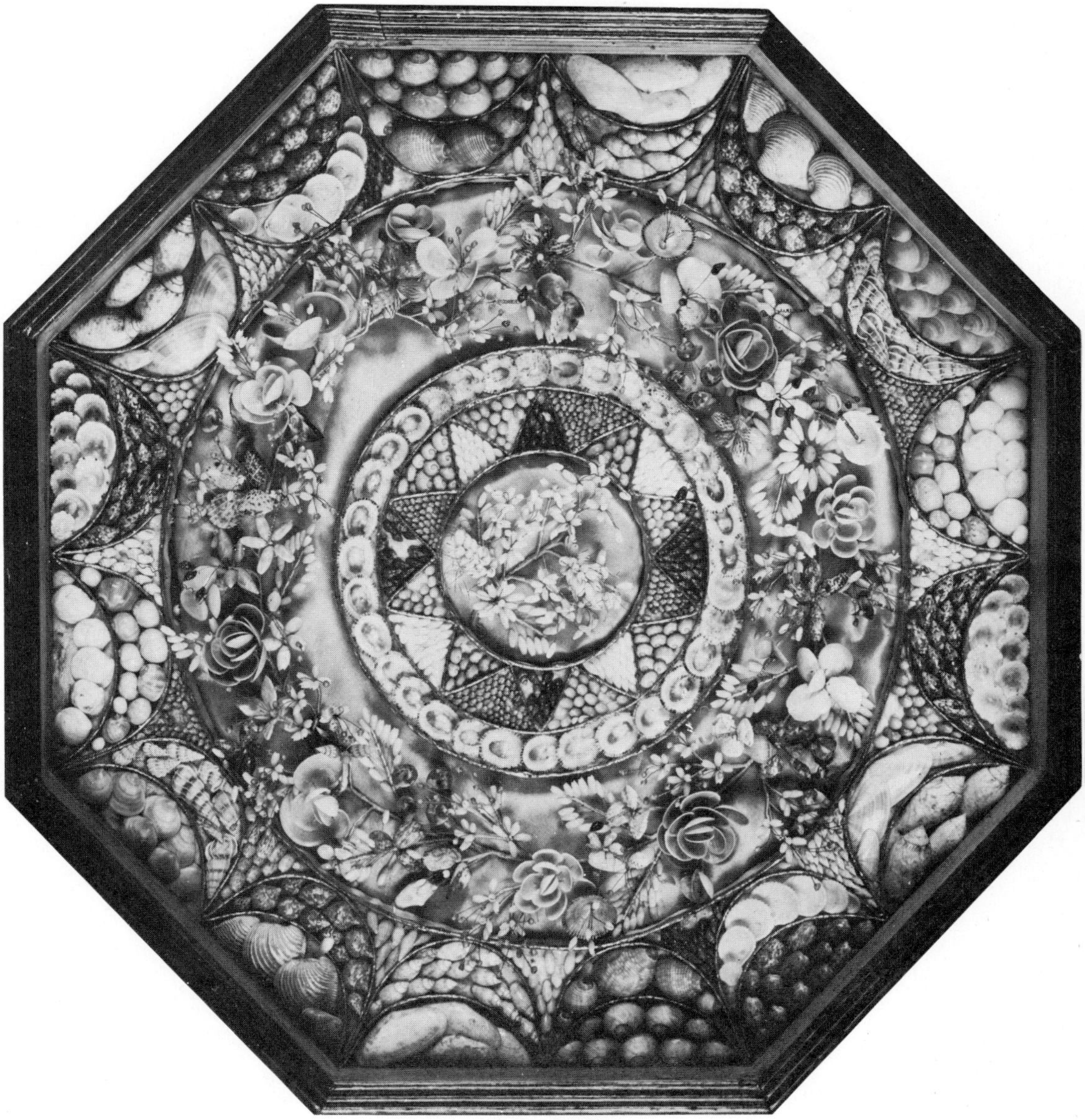

out to about 25 mm (1 in.) thick and trimmed to a square or rectangular shape. Again, do not attempt anything too large. Whilst still damp the clay can be cut into and impressed. When completely dry it will need firing and possibly later, glazing. If unfamiliar with these techniques, the reader is urged to consult other books which explain these processes in detail.

98 Picasso: *Still Life*. SPADEM, Paris. Copyright. The Tate Gallery, London

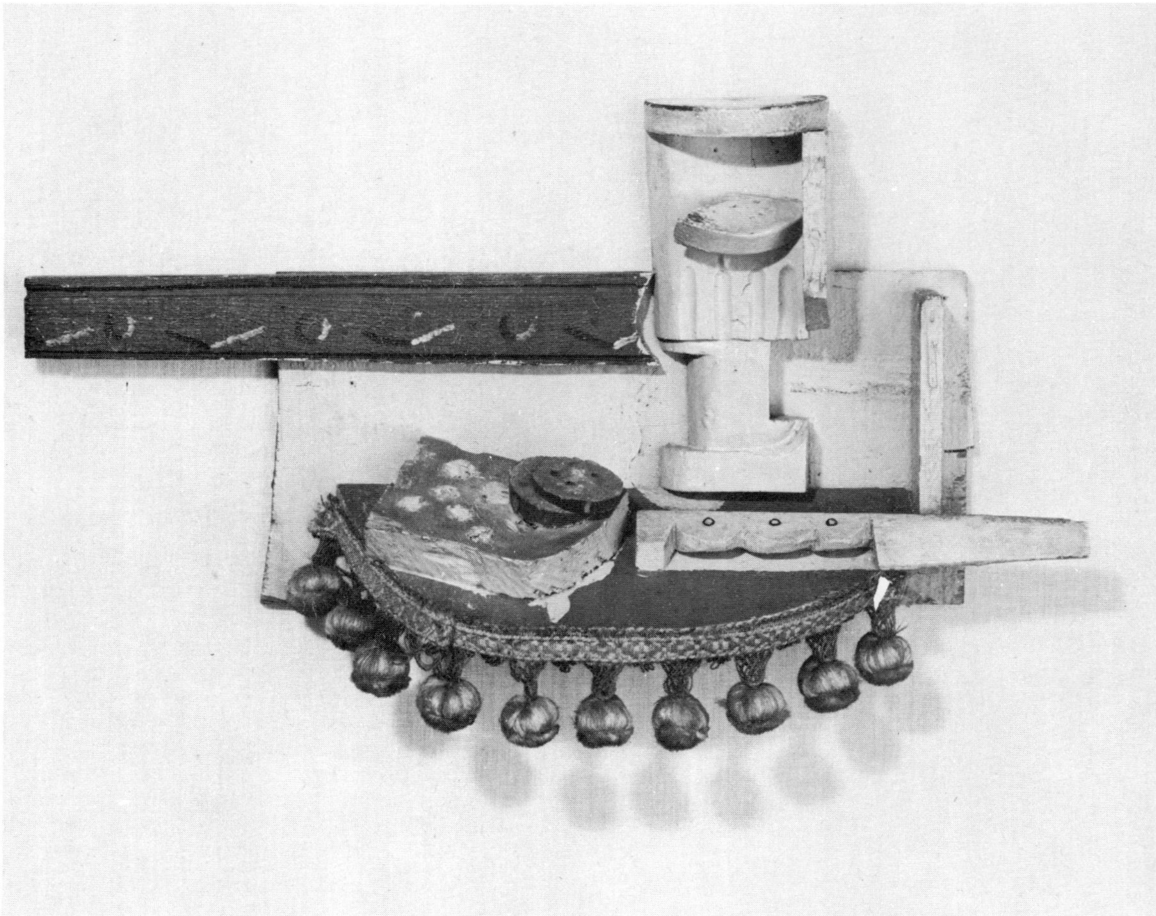

99 Peter Blake: *The Masked Zebra Kid* 1965. The Tate Gallery, London

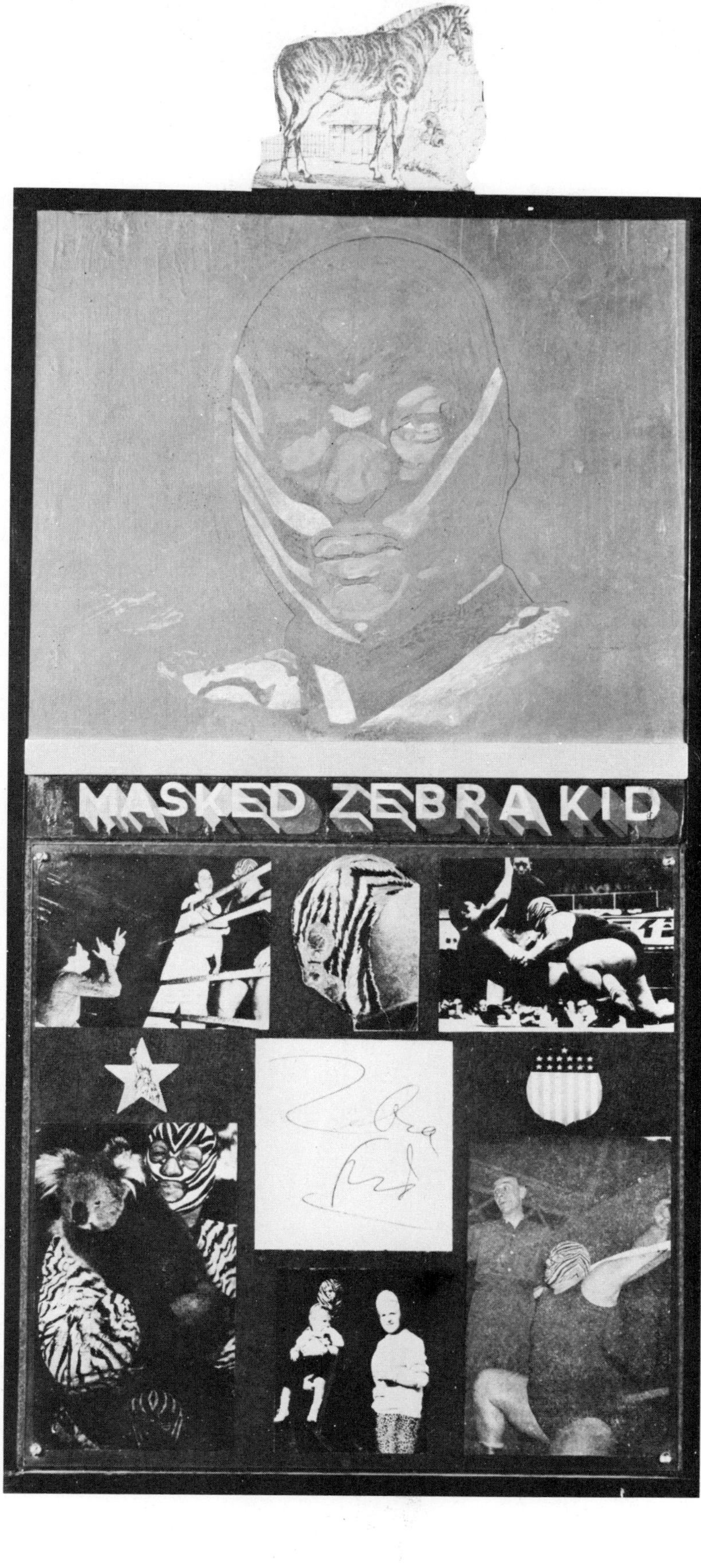
MASKED ZEBRA KID

100 Peter Blake: *Toy Shop*. The Tate Gallery, London

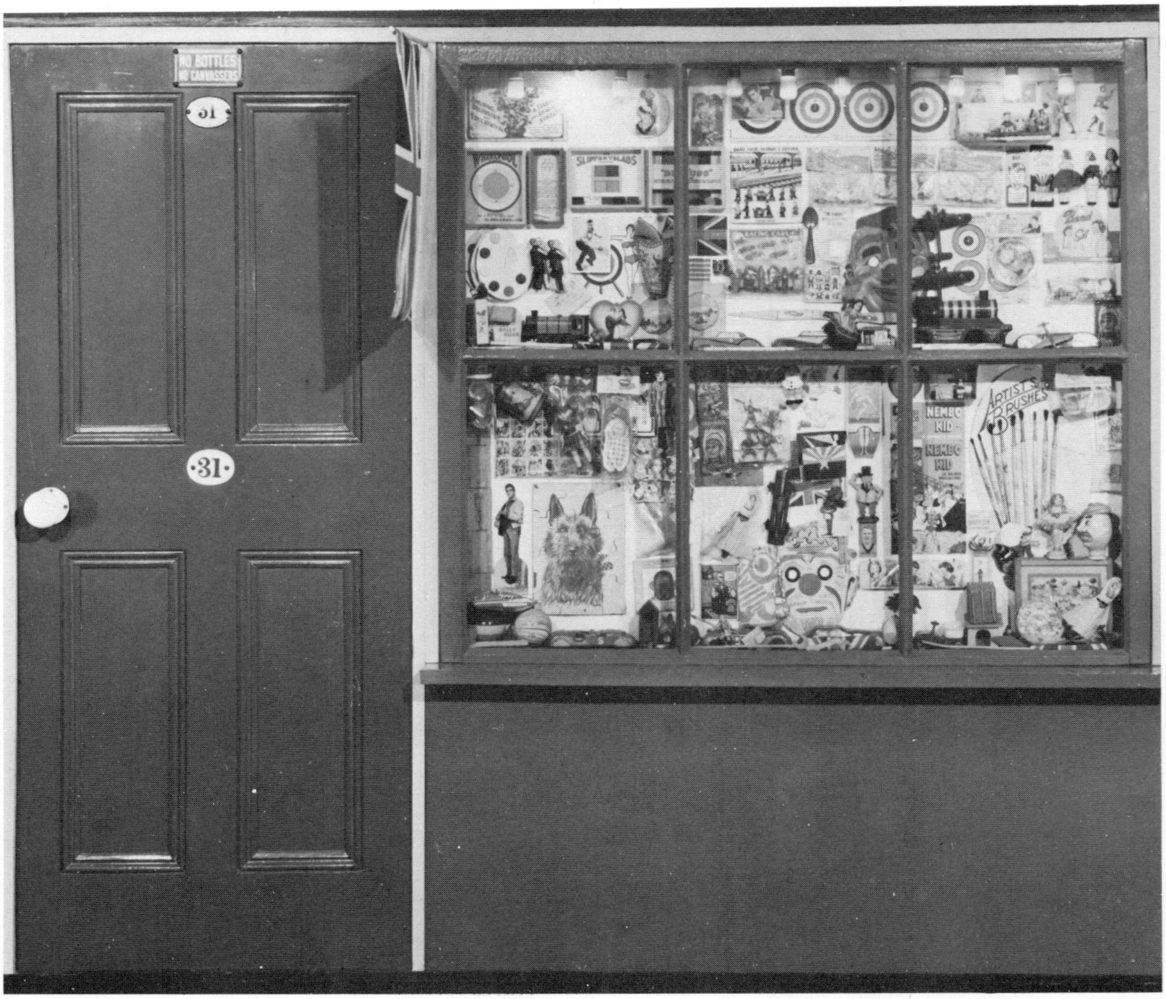

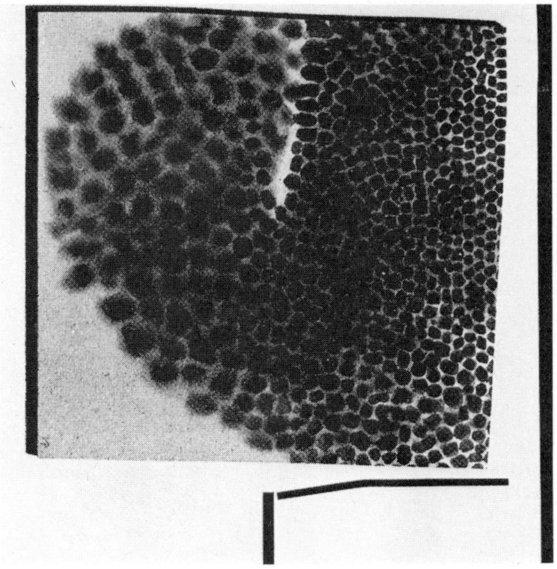

101 Victor Pasmore: *Black Abstract* 1963. Oil on board and incised formica relief.
The Tate Gallery, London

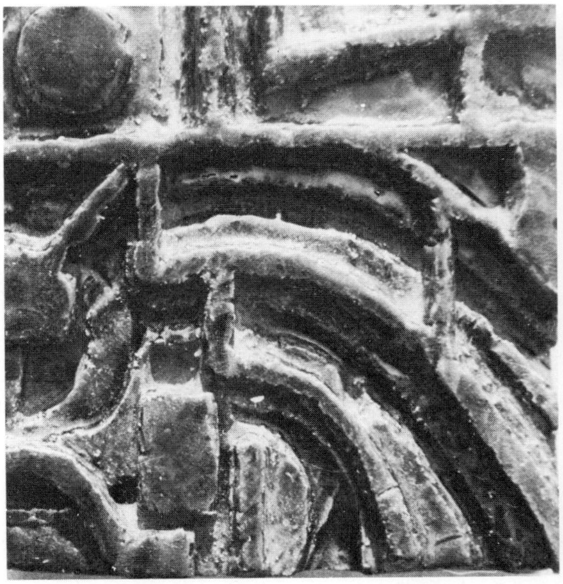

102 Glazed clay tile design

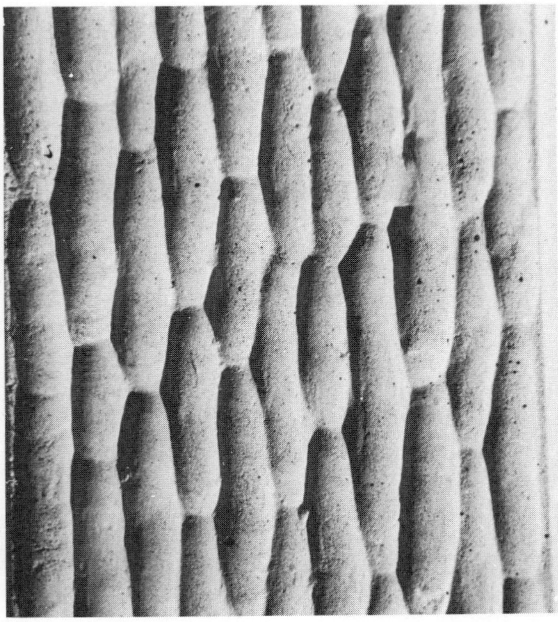

103 Modelled plaster surface

Plaster can also be used for texturing a surface and pictures can be made by impressing shapes into a thin plaster texture and allowing them to set, a similar technique to that described for the use of textured paint, see figure 8.

Polystyrene and tin are other suitable materials in this context, see section 5 and the text relating to the use of metals, page 74.

104 Ben Nicholson: *White Relief*.
The Tate Gallery, London

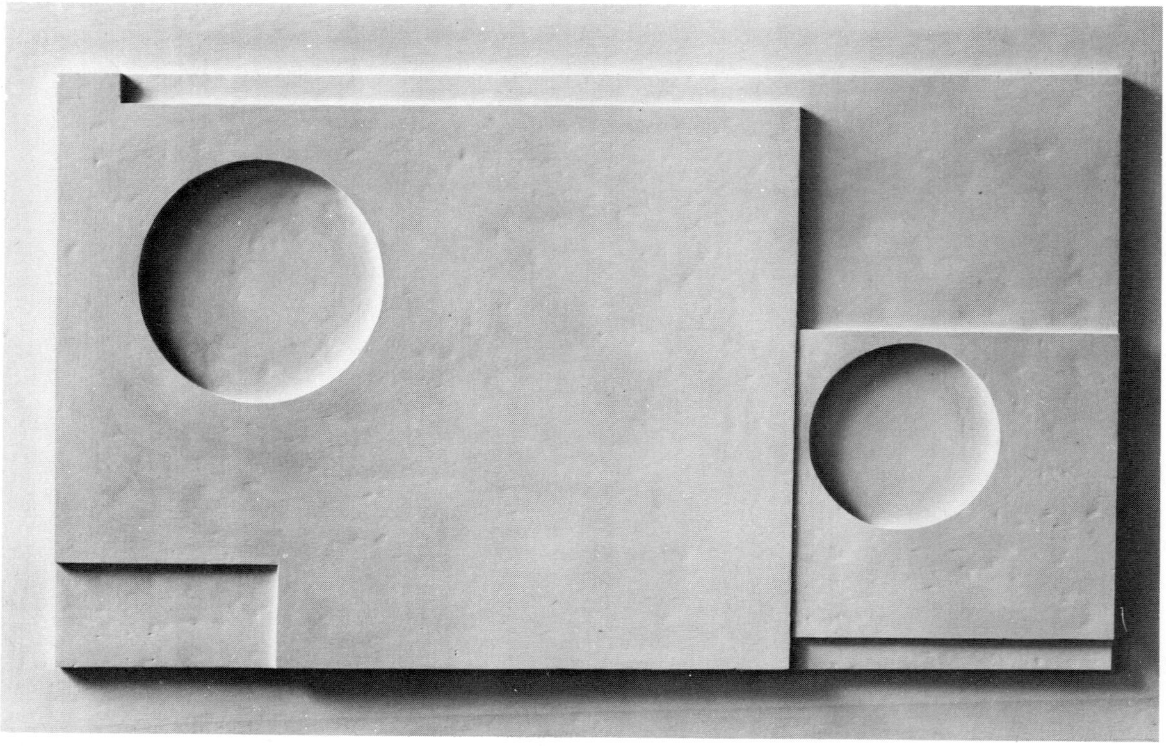

105 Jean Arp: *Constellations According to the Laws of Chance.* The Tate Gallery, London

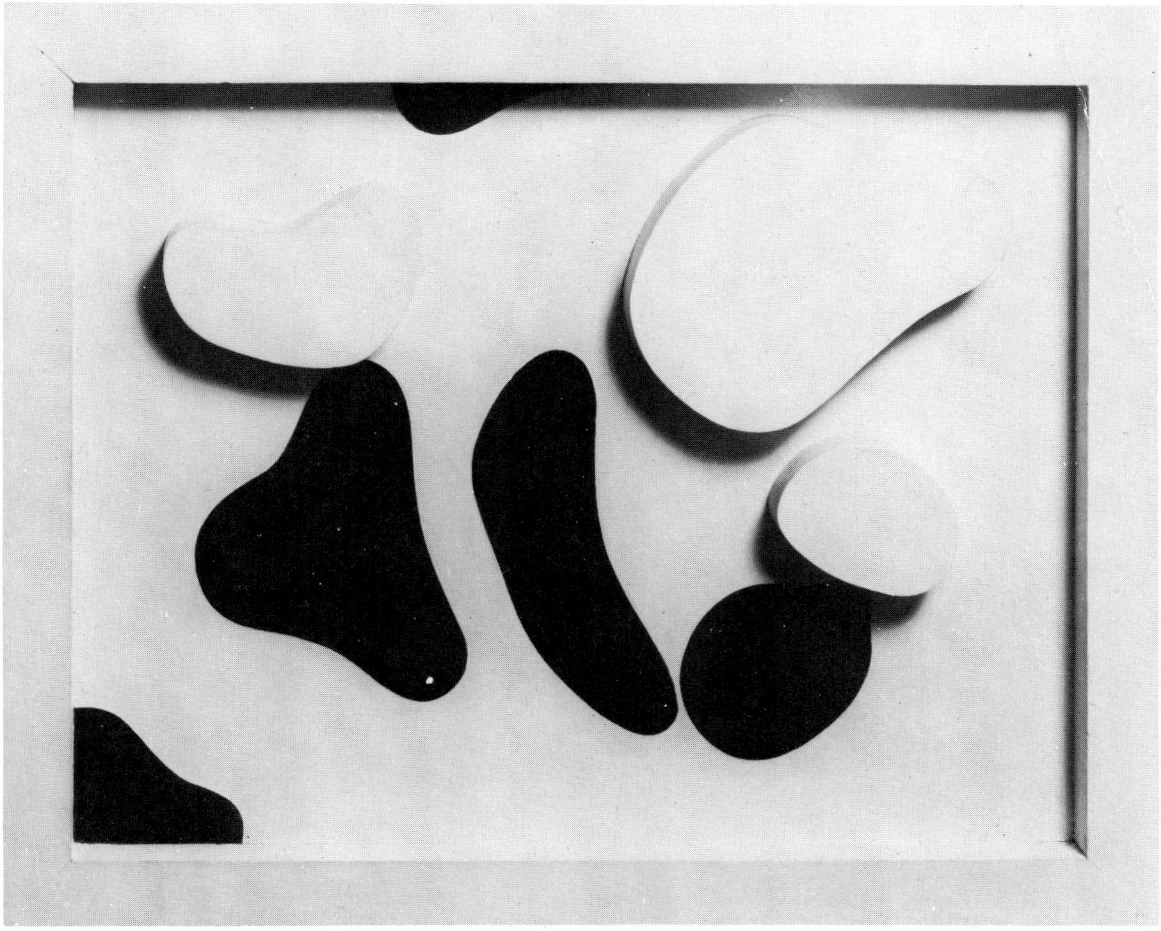

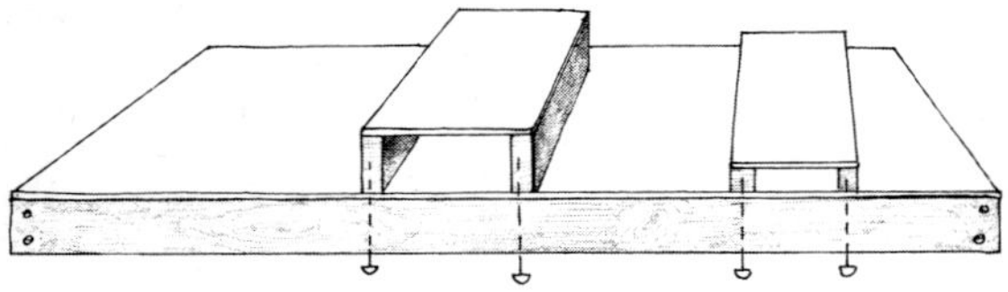

106 Constructing a special hardboard support (see also figures 39 to 43). The basic backed hardboard support can have raised parts built on to it

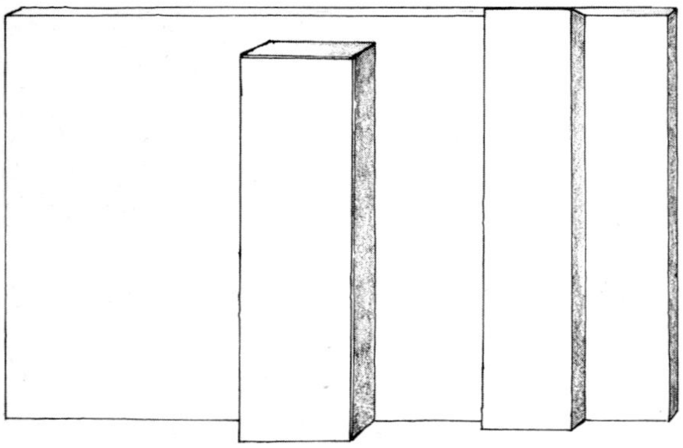

107 A vertical view of figure 106 showing how the two raised parts would protrude from the basic support

Constructing special supports

Large abstract works and perhaps those involving 'found' items may need supports which are a particular shape or design and these will require specially constructing. Wood or a board of some type will normally suit such work and this will need to be glued, screwed or nailed to a rigid, jointed wooden frame. The construction of the framework could take a form similar to that described for backing hardboard on page 39 and figures 39 to 43 and figure 106.

A support could be constructed with ledges running across it so that items can be placed or glued on to these. Other supports might involve an overhang at the top so that objects can be suspended in front of the picture surface.

These ideas will obviously require much forethought and planning for the work could become very complex, involving not only the design and carpentry of the support but also its preparation and painting as well as the colours, shapes and surfaces to be used in conjunction with it.

Technical notes

The following notes summarise general points and should be used in conjunction with the specific information given in appropriate sections of this book.

Materials

The most commonplace materials can be useful whilst art and craft shops and suppliers will offer a most extensive range of art materials. For some work, for example assemblage designs from waste cartons and containers, it will be necessary to collect materials over a period of time. If such work is to be undertaken with a large group or class, encourage each member of the class to contribute to the collection. A collection may be governed by specific ideas which are to be carried out, or it may be formed by a whole variety of interesting materials which it is thought could be useful for three-dimensional picture-making. As storage is often a problem, it is pointless to hoard material which is never going to be used. Many sources of materials have been outlined in the text and a comprehensive list of suppliers is included at the end of this book. Do not overlook the possibility of using remnants and offcuts or of combining a variety of materials. Offcuts, scrap and 'found' items can be suitably stored in large, strong cardboard boxes, the contents of which are clearly labelled on the outside. It is as well to ensure that adequate materials are available before beginning the work.

Equipment

The equipment will include a suitable support or backing on which to make the picture, as well as cutting tools and adhesives. The support may be of paper, cardboard, canvas, hardboard or plywood and its selection will depend on the type of work to be undertaken. Sharp scissors will cut a good many materials, so will a craft knife or safety razor-blade. Hardboard and wood can be cut with a hand-saw or tenon saw and polystyrene with a sharp knife or battery-operated cutter. PVA adhesive or *Marvin Medium* will suit most surfaces to be glued; other adhesives are mentioned below. The surfaces of some materials can also be engraved or incised in some way and for this drills, rasps, gouges and modelling tools may be required. A hammer, a staple-gun, steel pins and pliers are other useful items of equipment. Particular paints, brushes, varnishes and so on may be required according to the type of work and the materials used.

Adhesives

Most papers will stick adequately with a liquid glue such as *Gloy* or *Polycell*. PVA and other similar adhesives are extremely useful as they will stick a variety of materials, including polystyrene and thin wood. These adhesives can also be thinned with water for use with paper and as a protective clear varnish. Mixed media or work on a heavier support may require an impact adhesive such as *Copydex*, *Evostick*, *Bostik* or *Uhu*. Other suitable glues are mentioned where appropriate in the text and in the list of suppliers.

It is often easier to work with glue which has been poured into a shallow container or palette. Some glues will stain the surface of the work if accidentally spilt on it. Gluing the various parts of the design must therefore be done carefully. Ensure that adequate glue is used, particularly on the corners and edges of individual shapes. Some glues can be applied direct from the tube, others with a brush or small piece of cardboard or wood. Brushes used to apply PVA, *Gloy* or *Polycell* can be cleaned in water; this should be done immediately after use, before the glue has time to dry.

108 Some basic equipment

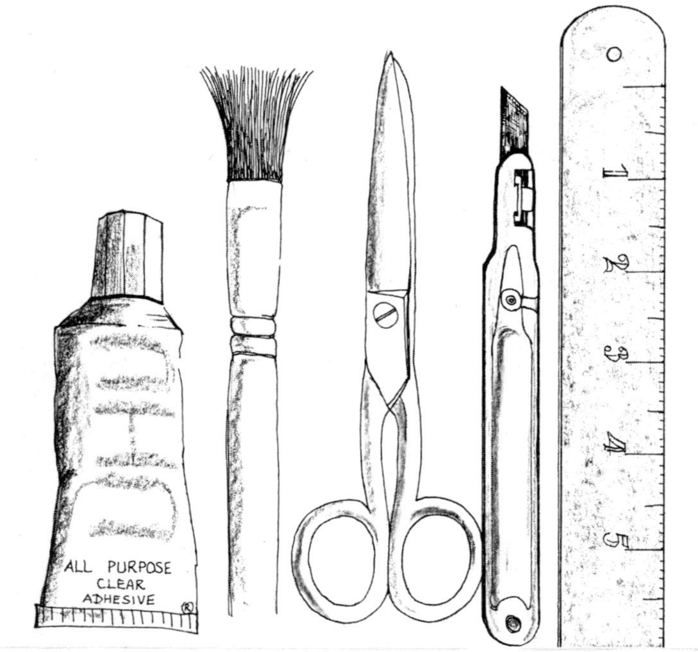

Work space

Creating three-dimensional pictures will often require a larger working space than that needed for painting or graphic work. Organise the space available so that maximum use can be made of it. Some space will be needed for the storage of work, when completed and whilst under construction. The more complex techniques may require special equipment and the availability of a work bench and electric power points.

Painting

The paint is selected according to its suitability for a particular surface or material. The work can be brush painted or sprayed by using a spray gun, spray diffuser, or aerosol cans of paint. Powder paint, poster paint and emulsion paints will suit paper, cardboard and hardboard surfaces, whilst gloss and enamel paints are better on glass, plastics and metals. Polystyrene must be painted with a water-based paint. Acrylic and PVA paints suit most surfaces, as does *Reeves Craft Paint*. Gloss, enamel and some spray paints will require turpentine substitute for cleaning up and rinsing brushes; other paints are easily diluted in water and those are recommended for use by children.

Staining and varnishing

Various stains are obtainable for use on wood, as are gloss and matt varnishes. *Ronseal* hardglaze polyurethane wood seal is useful for treating natural wooden surfaces. Clear varnishes are now available for most surfaces. The varnish may be applied with a soft, clean brush or sprayed from an aerosol can. Paper varnish, *Cryla No 1 Gloss Medium, Cryla No 2 Matt Medium* and thinned PVA medium are also useful.

Texturing

Many surfaces can be textured by painting them over with a thin coating of plaster or *Polyfilla*. Wood can be roughened with a rasp or coarse sandpaper and other textures can be made by mixing sand and other materials with paint, as described in section 2.

Overworking

Low relief designs in paper and cardboard can be overworked with various graphic techniques as well as fumage and brûlage.

Drying

It is essential that all glued work is allowed to dry out thoroughly before it is moved or painted. The storage of such work must therefore receive consideration. Similarly, painted work must be dry before it is varnished. Paint and varnish sprayed from aerosol cans must be allowed to dry before further coats are applied.

Mounting and display

Work which has been done on a paper support may need trimming. Mounts are most suitably made from thick card or board of a neutral colour. They should allow a slight boarder to the work. Heavier designs can be mounted on plywood or special frames devised, as discussed in section 4.

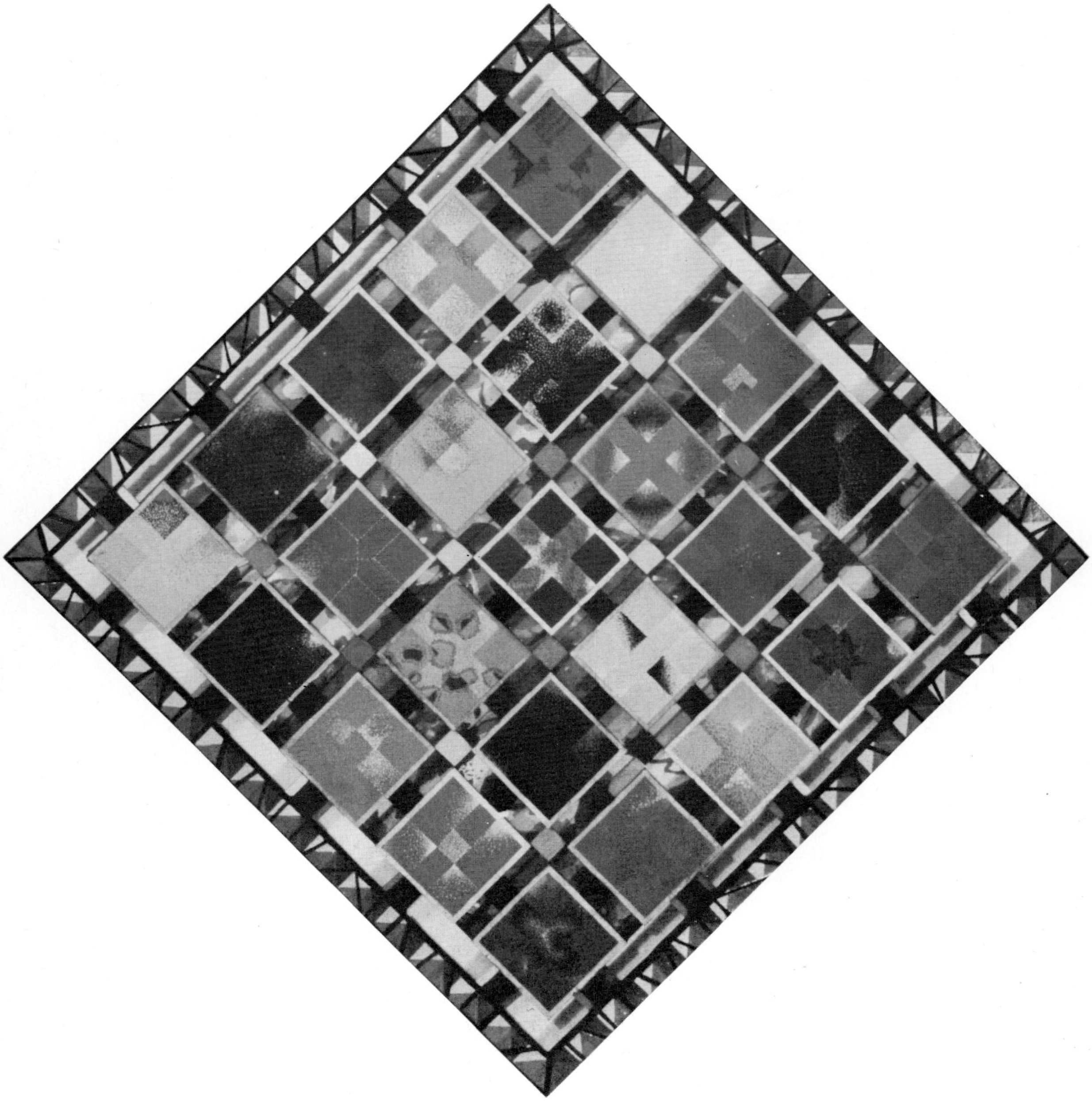

109 Richard Warner: *Keith's Delight*. Three-dimensional painting on layered wood. Chelsea School of Art

Further reading

Creative Corrugated Paper Craft Rolf Hartung, *Batsford, London*
Collage and Found Art Dona Meilach and Elvie Ten Hoor, *George Allen and Unwin, London*
Sculpture in Paper Ralph Fabri, *Watson-Guptil Publications, New York*
Creative Paper Craft Ernst Röttger, *Batsford, London*
Principles of Collage Brian French, *Mills and Boon, London*
The Technique of Collage Helen Hutton, *Batsford, London and Watson-Guptil, New York*
Creating in Collage Natalie D'Arbeloff and Jack Yates, *Studio Vista, London*
Introducing Fabric Collage Margaret Connor, *Batsford, London and Watson-Guptill, New York*
Introducting Seed Collage Caryl and Gordon Simms, *Batsford, London and Watson-Guptill, New York*
Designing with String Mary Seyd, *Batsford, London and Watson-Guptill, New York*
The Art of Assemblage W C Seitz, *The Museum of Modern Art, New York*
Creative Metal Craft Heinz Ullrich and Dieter Klante, *Batsford, London*
Creative Clay Craft Ernst Röttger, *Batsford, London*
Creative Wood Craft Ernst Röttger, *Batsford, London*
Introducing Constructional Art Edward Rogers and Thomas Sutcliffe, *Batsford, London and Watson-Guptill, New York*
Introducing Expanded Polystyrene Alan Barnsley, *Batsford, London and Watson-Guptill, New York*
A Concise History of Modern Sculpture Herbert Read, *Thames and Hudson, London*
The New Sculpture, Environment and Assemblages Ude Kultermann, *Thames and Hudson, London*
Surfaces in Creative Design Ernst Röttger, Dieter Klante and Friedrich Salzmann, *Batsford, London*
Basic Design—The Dynamics of Visual Form Maurice de Sausmarez, *Studio Vista, London and Van Nostrand Reinhold, New York*
A Concise History of Modern Painting Herbert Read, *Thames and Hudson, London*
The Nature of Design David Pye, *Studio Vista, London and Reinhold, New York*

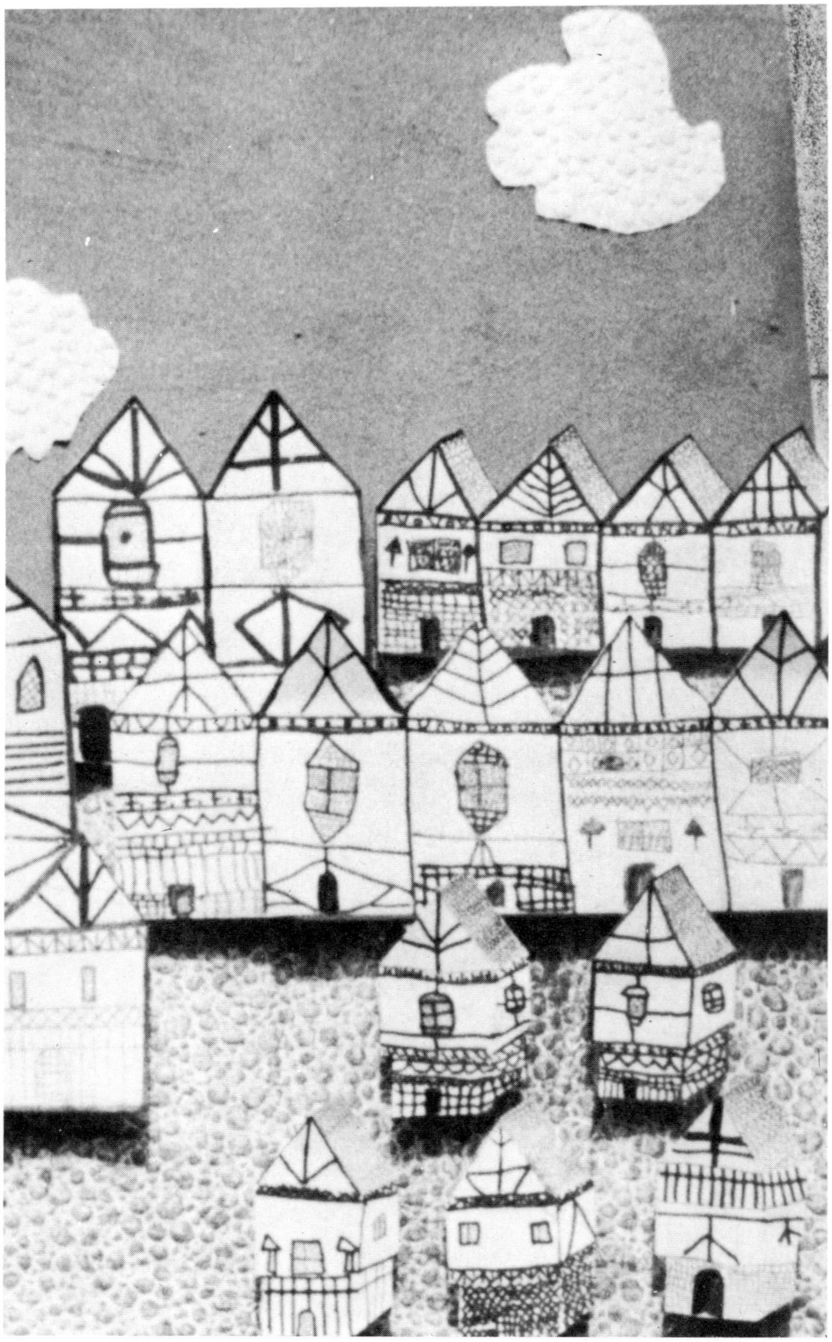

110 Detail of figure 37

Suppliers

GREAT BRITAIN

General art materials

Fred Aldous, Handicrafts Centre, 37 Lever Street, Manchester 760 1UX
E J Arnold (School Suppliers) Butterley Street, Leeds LS10 1AX
Arts and Crafts, 10 Bryam Street, Huddersfield HD1 1DA
Reeves Dryad, Northgates, Leicester LE1 4QR
Educational Supply Association, Pinnacles Harlow, Essex
Margros Ltd, Monument Way West, Woking, Surrey
Reeves and Sons Ltd, Lincoln Road, Enfield, Middlesex
George Rowney and Co Ltd, 10 Percy Street, London W1
Winsor and Newton Ltd, Wealdstone Harrow, Middlesex

Paper and cardboard

W & R Balston Ltd, Greens Fine Paper Division, Springfield Mill, Maidstone, Kent
F G Kettle, 127 High Holborn, London WC1
Grosvenor Chater and Company Ltd, 68 Cannon Street, London EC4
Paperchase, 216 Tottenham Court Road, London W7
Spicer Cowan Ltd, 19 New Bridge Street, London EC4
Strong Hanbury Company Ltd, Peterborough Road, Fulham, London SW7

Hardboard and timber

From local timber merchants and 'Do-it-yourself' shops

Expanded polystyrene

E J Arnold Ltd and Margros Ltd (addresses as above)
Baxendale Chemicals, Accrington, Lancashire
Elford Plastics, Elland, Yorkshire
Venestra International—Vencel Ltd, Erith, Kent

Rope, string, canvas and hessian

Russell and Chapple, Monmouth Street
London WC2
Euston Asbestos, Euston Road, London NW1

Embroidery materials

The Needlewoman Shop, Regent Street
London W1
Mace and Nairn, 89 Crane Street, Salisbury
Wiltshire
Christine Riley, 53 Barclay Street, Stonehaven
Kincardineshire AB3 2AR
Mrs Joan L Trickett, 110 Marsden Road
Burnley, Lancashire

Fabrics

Bradley Textiles, 15 Stott Street, Nelson
Lancashire
Tootal and Co Ltd, Oxford Street, Manchester
John Lewis, Oxford Street, London and
branches

Clay and plaster

Ferro (Great Britain) Limited, Wombourne
Wolverhampton WV5 8DA
Fulham Pottery Ltd, 210 New Kings Road
London SW6 4NY
Harrison Mayer Ltd, Meir, Stoke-on-Trent
ST3 7PX
Wengers Ltd, Etruria, Stoke-on-Trent ST4 7BQ

Balsa wood

Balsa Imports Ltd, 38 Bow Lane, Cannon Street
London EC4
Solarbo Ltd, Commerce Way, Lancing, Sussex

Adhesives

Gloy Multiglue: Gloy Schools Service
Association, Adhesives Limited, 8th Avenue
Works, Manor Park, London E12
Copydex: Copydex Limited, 1 Torquay Street
Harrow Road, London W2
UHU: Liberta Imex Limited, Liberta House
Scotland Hill, Sandhurst, Camberley, Surrey
Marvin Medium: Margros Limited, Monument
House, Monument Way West, Woking, Surrey
PVA Medium: George Rowney and Co
10 Percy Street, London W1
PVA Adhesive: Reeves and Sons Ltd, Lincoln
Road, Enfield, Middlesex

These and other glues such as 'Heavyduty' *Polycell, Bostick, Evostick, Unibond* and *Polybond* are available from good stationers or hardware stores.